KEEP YOUR FORK

The Best Is Yet To Come

Margie Melvin Long

with original artwork by Misty Town

outskirts
press

The opinions expressed in this manuscript are solely the opinions of the author and do not represent the opinions or thoughts of the publisher. The author has represented and warranted full ownership and/or legal right to publish all the materials in this book.

Keep Your Fork
The Best Is Yet To Come
All Rights Reserved.
Copyright © 2016 Margie Melvin Long
v3.0

Cover Photo © 2016 thinkstockphotos.com. All rights reserved - used with permission.

This book may not be reproduced, transmitted, or stored in whole or in part by any means, including graphic, electronic, or mechanical without the express written consent of the publisher except in the case of brief quotations embodied in critical articles and reviews.

Outskirts Press, Inc.
http://www.outskirtspress.com

ISBN: 978-1-4787-7962-9

Outskirts Press and the "OP" logo are trademarks belonging to Outskirts Press, Inc.

PRINTED IN THE UNITED STATES OF AMERICA

Dedications

For Tiffany

At the end of the day, let there be no excuses,
no explanations, no regrets.

For Michele

Thank you for being the love of my life and
always allowing me to follow my heart,
even when that means fantasizing
about completely unrealistic dreams!

For Linda Town

Mom, thank you for sending me the story
about the fork. If it hadn't been for you,
none of this would be possible.

Table of Contents

1. I Believe 2
2. Memorial Gardener 10
3. Tiny Dancer 22
4. The Happy Place 32
5. Tattoo on Your Heart 44
6. Father with a Capital F 58
7. The Witch 68
8. Bridge of Hope 84
9. Faith to Last a Lifetime 100
10. In the Moment 110
11. Fostering Faith 130
12. Return to Paradise 140
13. Miracle of Faith 158
14. End of the Line 176
15. Heaven on Earth 190
16. Criss-Crossing Dimensions 204
17. Worm Food 220
18. Everlasting Life 236
19. Imagine 248
    Bibliography 253

I Believe

A little faith will bring your soul to heaven, but a lot of faith will bring heaven to your soul.
—Dwight L. Moody

I BELIEVE

I believe.

It's astounding that two simple words can and do define a person. They certainly are critical to defining me.

I believe in God...though when I meditate and need to draw upon an image, it's female. I believe God is in me, *is* me. I believe that there is a difference between religion and spirituality...religion is for those who are afraid of going to hell; spirituality is for those who have been there and don't want to go back. I believe in an afterlife that is inclusive of all God's creations...big and small, believers and non-believers, animals and humans, saints and sinners. Since we were all created by God in His own likeness, He certainly wants all of His creations to return to Him after the physical body has passed.

I believe there is a heaven...I don't have to know where it is or what it looks like or what it will be like to reside there. All I need is that belief to wrap me in warmth and safety like a well-loved quilt.

I don't believe that God is a judgmental, cloud-sitting man with a white beard; as a recovering Catholic, that hasn't always been the case. My God is a constant presence in me, a spiritual being that needs no definition or image to be real and meaningful. That belief in God brings with it a belief in His promise to me: eternal life with Him in heaven.

Afterlife, heaven, the place we think of when we refer to our deceased loved ones looking down on us, that great unknown that has intrigued, confounded and in some cases divided us for centuries. Though we have the testimonies of those who claim to have had a near-death experience and describe it in great detail, we truly don't know what heaven is like…and there is great ambiguity for some as to whether it exists at all.

For those who believe, heaven offers the possibility and hope of reuniting with our deceased loved ones. But since this earthly experience is the only life we know, even those who believe in an afterlife are hell-bent on hanging on to it as long as possible. Death is frightening because it represents an end to the only life we know for sure. We leave memorials at gravesites and along the side of the road to mark the location of a loved one's moment of passage, we build shrines in our homes to those who have passed, scour websites dedicated to researching ancestry…all in an attempt to prolong our earthly connection. We write names on the back of old photos so that even future generations will not forget. Because above all else, we don't want our loves ones to be forgotten. And, of course, we ourselves don't want to be forgotten.

I BELIEVE

Dying is a very natural part of living. But for those who believe, our passing is not an ending but a beginning…a transition into a new life, which we call death. Faith offers hope and peace at the end of life's journey. There are many things that point us to a belief in the afterlife. For Christians, The Bible is full of various descriptions of what heaven will be and how we can be assured of spending eternity there with God. Through documented stories of near-death experiences, we hear about people who have seen and heard things that cannot be explained in human terms. Spiritual moments between earthly and eternal life…perhaps God giving us a glimpse of heaven before we get there. Through faith in this incredible concept, we are taken out of physical context and brought into the context of the spiritual as the soul journeys back to its Creator. He offers meaning, hope, comfort and understanding to those whose earthly life is ending. It is all about love—nothing more, nothing less. God loves each and every person He has ever created, warts and all. It is His wish that not one be lost. In all the experiences God allows His children to have, He is preparing to take them home to Himself. We all want to know what happens after we die. Various religions proffer diverse beliefs about what that looks like, and in the stories found in *Keep Your Fork*, you'll learn about many of them. Yet in spite of all that has been written about the afterlife, questions abound.

KEEP YOUR FORK

Where is Heaven? We refer to Heaven as up, as if in the clouds, where our loved ones watch over us. A bit of Bible trivia: the Hebrew word for heaven, Shamayim, is also the word for "skies."

What does Heaven look like? A city? A garden? A banquet? An amphitheater in the form of a celestial rose?

Is heaven a physical place? I think believers typically imagine heaven as a place because that's the only frame of reference we have based on our earthly experience. Thinking in terms of a place allows us to think of heaven as attainable and possible.

What happens to your body in Heaven? Or are we body-less souls—a bright, blissful spiritual union with God?

Heaven is a place both known and unknown, like this world but unlike it—a place of love and justice, big enough to accommodate all the souls in the world but open only to some. Heaven is a place or state of being impossible to describe in human language, where there is an infinite amount of time.

It is more comfortable for more skeptical believers to think of heaven as something that happens here on earth…in attempts at love or speaking truth or creating beauty or in contemplation of nature's beauty…

than it is to imagine another realm, built and populated and as real as this one. And in fact you have only to experience the birth of a child or a heart-stoppingly beautiful sunset to know that the perfection of heaven can in fact be caught in glimpses here on earth. Henry David Thoreau says "Heaven is under our feet as well as over our heads."

Heaven isn't about going to church for an hour on Sunday and then way off in the future you go to heaven. It's about doing what God asks us to do right now.

The trick to having faith in heaven is to do so in spite of the fact that it is, on the face of it, implausible. Even the testimonies we have of those who claim to have had a near-death experience are subjective and impossible to corroborate.

What will we see when we get to heaven? Those who had horrible lives on earth often imagine the opposite of their experience when they get to heaven. While those who lived well will picture something very similar to their earthly lives...only better. Since humanity began, we have imagined an afterlife as a place rather than a state of being, where we'll see our dead loved ones and do the things we love to do or what was impossible for us to do here on earth...all without consequence. Today there are no limits to what people imagine as heaven. We use heaven as a synonym for our most pleasurable activities…the ultimate day in the park, trip to a far-away land or a favorite meal.

Critics of the heaven-is-whatever-you-want-it-to-be philosophy say it ignores the most important thing about heaven: it's where God lives. Heaven is a privilege awarded to the righteous. The reward of living a good life should not be to have all the sex you want with like-minded angels or to eat what you want and not get fat; it should not even be to reunite and make amends with the people you've lost. It should be to revel in a union with God. Many of our visions of life after death fail to include God.

Keep Your Fork was born from the story of the same name, prompting Misty and I to begin our journey of capturing stories from as many perspectives as possible as to what Heaven is and will be. What became obvious as we left one interview after another is that there are almost as many perceptions of heaven as there are people. We want this book to be thought-provoking, comforting and uplifting. Everyone dies. Sooner or later every life that has come into being, long or short, will end. According to a Gallup poll, 85% of us believe in heaven, in spite of a growing disillusionment with organized religion. The idea is not to answer the questions but to raise them. The idea of heaven is unbelievable, yet to believe it is one of the most powerful sources of comfort and hope a human being might have.

I BELIEVE

Perhaps *Keep Your Fork* will add some paint strokes to a canvas we are all anxious to understand. The examined afterlife may influence how we spend our time on earth.

Margie Melvin Long

Memorial Gardener

*One generation passeth away,
and another generation cometh:
but the earth abideth forever.*
—Ecclesiastes 1:4

MEMORIAL GARDENER

Rodney Heinsohn is a burly teddy bear of a man, well manicured, soft-spoken and kind. He is also a funeral director, and we met when he helped the family make arrangements for my stepdaughter's funeral. His kindness, empathy and quiet professionalism led me to believe he would have a story that would be a great contribution to this book...and I wasn't disappointed. He was destined to excel in his field.

Rodney and I met at his suburban home for our interview. Before we even entered the house, he showed me around the front yard, which is filled with flowers. He pointed to one plant and said his aunt and uncle gave that to him when his parents died. His great-great grandparents gave that plant as a wedding present to his grandparents. That Chinese hollyhock is from his parents' garden, and that one is from his grandpa's garden, and that one over there is from his deceased uncle. The Shasta lilies came from the grandparents of little Henry right after he died in a car wreck. Rodney said he would be thinking of Henry that afternoon when he goes to the pond where they used to fish together. Being with Henry always reminded Rodney of himself as a child, being outdoors with his grandpa, fishing, helping him in the garden. As we moved into the house, he pointed out dried flowers from his mom's casket that hung framed in the living room. With a sad look on his face, he said it was a blessing they went together.

KEEP YOUR FORK

And in that house are lots of family furniture and mementos…lots of history.

Rodney is all about history…and family.

Inspired by the beauty and emotion I had seen in just a few short minutes, I was further moved when we left the house to sit in a shady spot in the backyard for our visit. There's a huge garden overflowing with flowers and vegetables, and one gets the feeling of being in the country even though Rodney's home sits in a densely-populated suburban neighborhood. He led me to a pergola-covered patio, hidden behind more foliage and shaded by mature fruit trees. It was there that I got to hear a beautiful story of life, death and the comfort of what lies beyond.

Rodney Heinsohn grew up in the funeral industry, not on the funeral home side as he is now as a funeral director, helping bereaved families lay their loved ones to rest…but on the cemetery side. His parents owned two cemeteries in Topeka, so at the ripe old age of 6 he was put to work mowing them. For close to 50 years now he's been involved in that environment, everything from mowing the grounds to digging the graves…they even had their own vault company to make the vaults. He came to Kansas City originally to attend a mortuary school program at a local community college. The intent was for him to

MEMORIAL GARDENER

come here to go to school and then ultimately go back home. His parents were going to retire, and his brother would do a lot of the outside maintenance work while Rodney took care of the business end of the cemeteries. Rodney actually intended to go back and ultimately add a funeral home to the family business. Ultimately he met and married a local girl who didn't share that vision, and his parents had an offer to sell. With some obvious nostalgia in his voice and a brief flash of melancholy crossing his face, he admitted that he regrets not going back...giving up to easily on his dream of having his own funeral home on his parents' property.

Rodney's parents died tragically together in a car crash. He told them goodbye as they were pulling out of his driveway, and a couple of hours later the state troopers knocked on the door. Rodney feels guilty because he had invited them to his home for the weekend. The night before was his sister's birthday, and the family gathered to celebrate. Within 24 hours, his parents got to be with all of their children and grandchildren. On one hand, if he hadn't invited them they wouldn't have had a chance to spend their last hours on earth with their loved ones. On the other hand, his invitation placed them in the wrong place at the wrong time. He believes God knew and had a hand in drawing them all together that weekend.

KEEP YOUR FORK

In the funeral business, there are people who work with the dead (embalmers) and people who work with the living (funeral directors who support families planning services for a loved one). When he started out he was on the preparatory and embalming side of the business, working nights before a day shift opened up. As the business grew, the staff became specialized. He had been in that little room day after day, night after night, and then an opportunity presented itself to become a funeral director. Some loved ones who come to the funeral home have a large family or church friends who support them; others have no one. In those cases, the funeral director is the only means of support available to the bereaved--a shoulder to cry on, a counsel for funeral protocol, a confidant. Being a funeral director may not be sexy, but it is far from dull or boring. Emotions are running high, and a death brings out the best or the worst in people. Families sometimes fight among themselves; Rodney has had to call the police to a funeral for outstanding warrants; there have been physical fights; he's had knives pulled on him; gunfights have broken out. There are times when arrangements have to be made for two rooms: separate rooms for two different sides of a family. But all have one thing in common...someone has transitioned from an earthly plane to the next. And Rodney believes "death comes as either a welcome friend or as a thief in the night."

MEMORIAL GARDENER

Everything he has done in his career has been caring about and for people. He is driven by a desire... no, a need...to continue respect for life into that next plane. There are many ministers and missionaries in the Heinsohn family, but he never felt called to a formal ministry in spite of his religious beliefs and values. Getting up and preaching to a crowd just doesn't suit him. But I can tell you from having worked with Rodney, what he does is a form of ministry.

Death does not frighten Rodney, who says the deceased is still a person. Their life as we know it is over, but there's another dimension out there. The deceased has made their choices at that point as far as their own faith and afterlife. They've transitioned to whatever it is they believe is next. The job of the funeral director and his staff is to help the family, and of course they work with families of all faiths. Rodney sometimes finds it challenging not to transfer his own beliefs to the deceased. He says, "Everybody knows God at the time of death. There are no atheists in foxholes in the military."

There is an afterlife for Rodney, and he calls it heaven. It's glorious, better than what we have on earth, a life without pain. The spirit will have left the body, but as the Bible says, you have a new body, a new heaven and a new earth. He hopes it will be a big vegetable garden or flower garden he can tinker in all day. Not that we'll have to grow food in heaven, but because he gets so much pleasure and joy from working in the garden, his heaven would certainly include gardens. Some of his most spiritual moments have occurred outdoors. He's been in the mountains and has seen the aspen leaves and the elks bugling. You sit and listen to the babbling brook and sit on the mountainside and close your eyes and listen to the gentle wind blowing through. Your senses are all engaged: your vision of the glorious sights around you, smelling the pine and hearing the wind blowing and the turkeys gobbling. He's seen the beautiful snow-capped mountains and herds of elk walking and loping deer. He wonders if heaven might be a combination of those experiences. He hopes there are elevations like mountains and snow-covered peaks and beaches below. Yet he hopes that everybody's idea of how they envision heaven will come true. Not everybody loves the mountains, not everybody loves gardening. If you love scrapbooking, he hopes there's a scrapbooking section for you to enjoy. If you were forced to do something you didn't like on earth, that won't be in heaven. Heaven should be a place of pleasure and peace and relaxation, not of torment and misery.

He also believes in hell because, "I'd like to think there'd have to be a place for some of the people's ill doings on humanity. For what they've done there'd have to be a special place for them and a nice place for

MEMORIAL GARDENER

the good." Rodney believes in a moral compass that teaches that there are consequences for our actions. From a biblical standpoint, Rodney says if you're going to believe in heaven, you have to believe in hell. Why would you believe in one but not the other?

But that having been said, heaven isn't a reward for behavior. It's the result of a faith-based decision. You can't say you believe in God but then go out and rob a bank and be a menace on society as if believing in God allows you to get away with it. You can't have it both ways. If you have the values and beliefs in your heart, your life should demonstrate that. No one is perfect; we all make mistakes, but we are forgiven. Based on our faith in God, we strive to do better, we lose that desire to do bad things, and we want to live up to all that faith entails. That faith carries over to his professional life, and in fact I believe it's a large part of what makes him so good at his job. He's seen people come in who claim to be atheists and don't want any type of religious ceremony. There is hatred in their values and their heart. You can hear it in their emotions.

When Rodney's parents were killed in the car crash and he was talking to his pastor, one of the things that came up is how people without faith get through something like that. If you knew that was the true and that you were never going to see that person again, how much harder and difficult it would be. The belief that we'll see them again is what gets people through. You believe this person who's now transitioned is in a much better place. That allows Rodney to have comfort so he's not looking at each situation, each death, as bad. There's nothing but the respectful preparation of the deceased that they can do to soften the situation for the family and ease their pain in even a minimal way. In spite of his extensive experience with the business of death, he waited to see his own parents until after the embalmers had worked on them.

He shared the story of a family whose only son was killed in car crash. In their overwhelming grief, they didn't know where he was with his faith. A minister came to the funeral and told them he was on his way home from church and witnessed the crash that killed their son. He didn't die instantly, but the minister could tell he wasn't going to make it. He asked him if there was anything he could say or do for him, that he was a minister. He asked if his life was there he wanted it to be and talked to him about faith. Their son told him he was a believer and that he knew where he was going. His parents didn't know that…they knew only that a policeman arrived at their door with a devastating message. What the minister shared with them gave them great comfort.

Early in his career, Rodney met a man named Ron whose wife had divorced him six months prior and

MEMORIAL GARDENER

whose son had been killed by a gunshot. He was contemplating taking his own life when a second son was sent to prison...which threw him further into despair. Ron kept coming by to visit with Rodney, telling him he didn't think he wanted to live. Rodney gave him a hug and told him to hang in there, but it kept getting worse. Rodney suggested he go to a psychiatrist...he'd been there. How about talking to a minister? He'd tried that as well with no relief, but he kept coming back to Rodney. Finally Rodney asked why he kept coming back to him when he'd been to all available means of professional help...doctors and counselors and ministers, people who have gone through years of school and training...and he told Rodney, "They tell me how I *should* feel, you let me tell you how I *do* feel." Ron and Rodney have been friends for over 20 years, and he eventually started to get his life back together. He met a new woman and had a New Year's Eve party to which Rodney was invited. At one point in the evening Ron silenced everybody and told them Rodney had saved his life...if it wasn't for him, Ron would be dead. It was the best compliment Rodney will ever get, and it humbled him to a greater degree than he'd ever imagined.

While the guest of honor is deceased, funerals are for the living. No one wants to see their loved one placed away forever knowing how much tragedy and trauma they had to go through. Rodney can't fix everything or erase the pain, but he can soften things and remove some of their bitterness. When the deceased is a young person who dies tragically like my stepdaughter, Rodney provides personal support as well as helping with final arrangements that will provide some measure of comfort for those left behind. For an older person, a funeral can be a time of celebration rather than mourning.

When it's Rodney's time to cross over, he looks forward to reuniting with relatives, especially his parents. He's curious to see if they blame him for their deaths… because he will always blame himself. His mom had been having some health problems that would potentially cause the loss of her eyesight. Rodney had prayed that wouldn't happen…and it didn't.

Rodney and his wife had six miscarriages before they had their only child. He knows he'll get to see those little boys and girls. He knows because the Bible tells him so: blessed are the children for theirs is the Kingdom of Heaven.

He wants to see little Henry and his grandparents, who gave him his love of gardening and fishing. He's sure that Henry will be there to greet him with a couple of fishing poles and some bait.

Rodney has surrounded himself with his family in the

nature that he loves. His yard is his way of keeping them with him. Reuniting in heaven will be an easy transition….he has already created his own heaven on earth.

Tiny Dancer

An angel is dancing in heaven.

TINY DANCER

Names changed to protect anonymity

A typical Midwestern fall day, sunny and warm. A beautiful young woman sits at a stoplight, texting love notes to her husband of 18 months. A speeding car slams into the rear end of her car, propelling her into the intersection and killing her instantly.

That story is horrific, but this is not her story. This is the story of a mother trying to explain heaven to her child.

Imagine that you are the older sister of that young crash victim. Fast forward through the phone call telling you that your only sibling is dead, leaving you to be the messenger to both of your parents...and your 7-year-old daughter. Your precious, innocent child who has now lost her best friend in the world. This is their story...a story of loss, love and a search for solace in the afterlife.

Kristina* and her sister Brittany* were three years apart, and as children and teenagers experienced the normal sibling dramas. Brittany wasn't the typical tagalong little sister but instead revealed herself as a toddler to be an individual with a strong personality and very definite ideas about how things should be. Yet she also looked up to Kristina and sought to be her equal...especially in her passion for dance. As young adults, they forged a close friendship and planned to raise their children together. Brittany's death ended those dreams.

When Madison* was born, Brittany was in that between-college-and-the-real-world space…not yet having found her footing or a solid direction for her future. She was able to become Madison's nanny for the first several months of Madison's life, and a bond was formed that would never be broken. They weren't just aunt and niece; they were best buddies and in many ways grew up together. Sleepovers, holidays, shopping trips, picnics…whatever they could do together. Brittany would change Madison's clothes several times a day and do photo shoots…her own living doll.

While both sisters got teaching degrees, Kristina entered a classroom and Brittany eventually opened her own dance studio…a lifelong passion and a dream fulfilled. Madison seemed destined to follow her mom and her aunt into the world of dance, and it was made more special when she was able to dance at Aunt Brittany's studio.

On that fall day, Kristina picked Madison up from school and took her home to deliver a message no mother should have to share with her child. Her beloved Aunt Brittany, her best friend in the world, was gone forever. As is the case with most young children, death had touched Madison only briefly...with the death of her great-grandmother. Old and in poor health, her passing wasn't a surprise and was easily explained to and accepted by Madison. But how does a 7-year-old process the permanent loss of someone so young and vital, someone you had said goodbye to only two nights before at the dance studio?

Madison was born an old soul, extremely bright and inquisitive, reading by the time she was 3. She likes things black and white and wants concrete answers to all of her questions. Kristina, being not only her mom but also a teacher, had always been able to meet that expectation. Until now.

In the hours immediately following Brittany's death, Madison began to wonder where Brittany was "right now", and what's happening to her? What will they do to her body? Kristina tried to answer her factually and simply, but had to ask herself: do I take her to see Brittany or make the decision for her that she doesn't want to remember her that way, even to say goodbye? Her great-grandmother had a funeral and burial, so she was somewhat familiar with that process. But Brittany was going to be cremated. How do you explain cremation to a child? Kristina told her "there's a special room that's very hot so that the body just goes away"...how that's just her body she needed on earth, but "we know that's not her anymore." Madison seemed to accept that, but then began to wonder why Brittany doesn't need her body anymore. Where is she if she's not in her body? So the discussion naturally moved to heaven. A child's innocent, literal perspective on life brought questions like what does it look like? and where is it?

Kristina wants to instill an accepting nature in her children, so over Madison's seven years, they had talked a lot about a person having two selves: your inner self and your outer self. Kristina was able to use that concept to try and explain what happens to a person when they die. They had talked about inner beauty and not judging people by what they look like but by how they act. Madison understands that how you act comes from inside and how you look is on the outside. So Kristina used that foundation to give a name to that inner self: the soul. Your body is what you look like on the outside, but it's the inner you…your soul… that makes you who you are. And you can't see that. Your soul is the part of you that makes you a fun person, that makes you a smart person, that makes you a kind person. That's inside of you. It's not the body that makes you that way. While that was still not the concrete answer she craved, she could begin to connect some dots because she and her mom had always talked about the inside and outside selves. Kristina wanted to be sure Madison understood that Brittany's soul is the part that knows when Madison is happy or sad, or sees that she won an award or that can comfort her when she's feeling blue. It's still abstract, but she seemed to understand.

Having this discussion with your child would be hard for anyone, but Kristina wasn't sure of her own beliefs. She had no concrete answers for her child to comfort and reassure her; and as a mother, that was intolerable. How do I reassure my child without showing her some of my doubts?

Through the death of her sister and having to put her own grief on the back burner as she led her daughter into these uncharted waters, Kristina had to confront her own beliefs…and doubts. Whereas heaven hadn't entered her pragmatic world, it was now staring her in the face with big brown eyes filled with tears. She wanted very badly (read: needed) to believe there was a life after this so that she would someday see Brittany again. Processing it through with Madison and reassuring her, Kristina was trying to reassure herself as well. Many of the innocent questions posed were answered honestly with 'I don't know". Having to admit to your child that you don't have all the answers is horribly discomfiting and frightening for a child. As parents, they look up to you as the know-everything-make-everything-better people. And Kristina couldn't make this better.

Faith is a daunting concept for adults, so explaining it

to a child is extremely difficult. But this was so important for Kristina and Madison. The faith in an unknown afterlife is what got them through…the hope and promise of seeing Brittany again. Kristina explained that she couldn't tell Madison exactly what it looks like; this is one of those things that no one really knows until they get there. And since they can't tell us once they're there, you have to wait to get there to know for sure. "It's just one of those things you have to believe without seeing. You just have to believe it even though you can't see it." Because Madison needs to have the right answer for everything, that answer didn't satisfy her. So there were lots of tears…for both mother and child. Kristina said, "I want to answer her questions, and I can't."

Being the inquisitive child that is her nature, Madison had more questions as time passed. She and her mom would talk about Brittany being able to see and hear. Kristina encouraged her to talk to Brittany, to tell her how she's feeling. Madison created a special journal where she could write notes to Brittany and to recall special memories they shared. "Talk to her Madison… she can hear you," her mom encouraged. Of course this brought more questions. Madison now knew that Brittany's body was not here anymore and that she may or may not have a body in heaven…so how can Brittany see me if she doesn't have eyes? She doesn't have ears, how can she hear me? So Kristina told her eyes and ears are what we need here on earth, but everything is different in heaven. Without a body, what does she look like? Another "I don't know" is all Kristina could offer, but she did share her belief that you look the same as someone else would remember you. Madison got very, very upset when she heard that...almost panicky...because her mom had told her she'd be much, much older when she goes to heaven, and she said "Brittany won't even recognize me. I'll be an old person and she'll still be young and pretty and she won't know who I am!" Reassurance, such as it could be, came with her mom's belief that in heaven everyone sees each other how they remember them from here on earth. Brittany will see Madison as she was at 7 years of age. And of course, she's going to be watching as Madison changes and grows, so she'll know. That was the worst moment... she was so scared that Brittany wouldn't recognize her when they met again in heaven.

As the months passed, there was less talk of heaven. It may be that Kristina satisfied (or pacified) her for now, or perhaps she realized she wasn't going to get the answers she wanted so she just stopped talking about it. But for a long, long time she would talk to Brittany at bedtime; and it was a private time between niece and aunt. She didn't want anyone else there and would stop talking if her mom would come down the hall toward her own room.

Kristina had never been forced to confront her own

KEEP YOUR FORK

beliefs about heaven and admits even now that she has a lot to figure out. She feels Brittany's presence and believes Brittany is still with her. But she doesn't think Brittany is in another place, a place we call heaven, but rather is here with her and others who loved her. Madison wants it to be a very concrete place, you go there and this is what it's like. A place where people look like people, you're here and then you go someplace else. But for Kristina it's more abstract than that, and that makes it hard because she's left to wonder: will I actually get to see her again?

While Madison is encouraged to talk to Brittany, she's angry that Brittany can't talk back. How does a 7-year-old understand that her beloved aunt is still with her in her heart…when all she wants is to hug her and hear her laugh? Kristina can explain again and again that Brittany knows when she's feeling excited and happy about something that happened at school or when Madison is missing her. She knows when Madison is sad or proud or angry. But it's hard for her to talk to Brittany when she's not talking back.

They still talk often about memories, and with time it's less painful to do so. Madison realizes they'll always talk about Brittany…she's part of their life.

In Madison's little 7-year-old world, it is a reality that someone can be gone forever without warning. She said goodbye to her aunt at the dance studio on Wednesday night and never saw her again...ever. Kristina continues to find notes written from Madison to Brittany...I love you Brittany. So if Kristina is right, Brittany knows she is loved and missed by a beautiful little girl whose life was forever changed on that fall day. The day her innocence was stolen along with her aunt's life.

One thing is for sure: both Kristina and Madison are counting on dancing with her again one day.

Recipe for Peace

Ingredients
1 cup of friendship
1/2 cup of hope
2 cups of love
5 tbsp of respect
1/2 cup of kindness
1 cup of joy
3 tsp of understanding
1 1/2 cups honesty

Directions
- Mix friendship, love, and kindness in a large bowl. Add understanding a few drops at a time. Then stir in honesty and joy for good firm dough. Sprinkle half of respect over it and mix well.
- Pour into a cake pan and bake at 350°F. When it is ready, pour the hope and the rest of respect on top and share with everyone you know.

The Happy Place

May I be the medicine for those who are sick,
A partner for those who are lonely,
A bridge for those who need to cross over,
And a light for those who are blind.
   —Buddhist Prayer

THE HAPPY PLACE

Barb Abernethy had a life-changing event in 2009 that caused her to question her whole belief system. Looking back, she feels guilty that she ever questioned her faith, but she can't deny that she did. Because in 2009, her 22-year-old daughter Ashley died of a rare and aggressive sinus cancer.

Barb is a devout Catholic and believes in eternal life...and she calls that Heaven. The vision of what she thinks Heaven will be like has changed over the years. When she was little she had so many questions. Her mom would say, "You'll find out when you get to Heaven". Barb wanted to know right then, but says she wasn't ready to leave her friends and family in order to find out...so she settled for imagining. Her dad went to Heaven when she was just 8 years old. In her childish innocent imagination, he was probably having a great time...telling stories, fishing, and she'd like to believe he could see again as he had been blind the last several years of his life from complications of diabetes. She thought if she went to Heaven then, at age 8, she could eat ketchup bread and peanut M&M's all day as there would be an abundant supply. And in her vision, it was always summertime in Heaven.

As she got older her imagination shifted to a peaceful existence where everyone is always happy. It's light and white with beautiful music. It's always blue skies and warm breezes. The often-described image of

KEEP YOUR FORK

Pearly Gates and roads of gold seem too formal and ornate for Barb. Since Jesus seemed like such a simple man with a simple philosophy, she imagined Heaven that way as well.

When Ashley was diagnosed, Barb knew it was going to be a battle…but she never doubted they'd win. She prayed for a miracle, and a miracle is what she expected to receive. After all, they had God on their side.

Four months into their seven-month battle, doctors found a new tumor. As a mom, Barb asked about next steps, how they're going to treat it. And the doctor, you could tell by her face, told her Ashley is "incurable." Barb asked how much time her child had left, and the doctor had to admit that she didn't know because she had never dealt with sinus cancer. It might be months, or it could even be a few years. While Barb demanded more answers…answers she knew the doctor was unable to give…Ashley just wanted to "get the hell out of there." Her mom followed her and they held hands in the parking lot. Ashley stopped and said, "Mom, what are we going to do?" Barb replied, "Well, we're going to pray. Pray for a miracle." She was shocked when Ashley said, "No, I mean it's not fair. I get to go to the happy place and you and dad and Kelsey have to stay here." She had a calmness about her. She was upset but was completely calm. She seemed almost

THE HAPPY PLACE

excited...like she was going off on a vacation that her loved ones weren't able to go on. Barb swears they never referred to heaven as "the happy place" in their home; it was always heaven. That was Ashley's impression of it, an impression she came to on her own. As Barb thinks back on it, she realizes Ashley had been thinking about this. It didn't just pop into her head. And from that moment on, all prior images and expectation of heaven fell away, and heaven became simply "The Happy Place."

When it became apparent Ashley's transition was near, she was moved to hospice care. The first day, Mizzou was playing KU. Barb's friends came with her and brought beer to watch the game. Ashley slept, but every now and then she'd pop up and ask who was winning. At that point the tumor was pressing so hard on her vocal chords that she couldn't talk very well so it was a struggle for her to communicate. But she liked having everybody there; a friend even brought her dog there. To her it was everybody sharing stories. End of life transition is more somber in a hospital setting; in hospice, it's more like home. She was there Saturday, Sunday, Monday and died Tuesday afternoon. Every day that room was filled with people...friends laughing and crying. Barb is sure she enjoyed that transition, knowing she was with people she loved and cared for.

KEEP YOUR FORK

After Ashley passed, Barb questioned whether Heaven was indeed real. Sure, she says, "I spent my whole life believing and subsequently passing that belief on to my children; but now that I had a child who was supposedly there, was she really? What if I was wrong?" She struggled because she felt like she was betraying her entire belief system. A friend with whom she shared her doubts suggested she read the book *90 minutes in Heaven*. Reading that book reassured Barb that Heaven was definitely real, and she was suddenly at peace again knowing that Ashley made it to the "Happy Place". Now Barb feels confident that Heaven is full of smiling people...happy people..."joyful happy people everywhere." Like Ashley always said, life is too short to be anything but happy.

When Barb joins Ashley in heaven, the first person she wants to see is Jesus "of course, because He is the reason we are there!" When asked what specifically she'd say to Jesus, she calls to mind the song "I Can Only Imagine" by MercyMe. Barb can't listen to it without crying. That's how she imagines it will be when she makes it to Heaven.

Then of course, she'll just want to hug Ashley and tell her she DID make it to the "Happy Place", and then she'd go check on her dad.

THE HAPPY PLACE

Barb Abernethy is one of the kindest, most giving people you could ever meet, and yet even she believes she'll be better in Heaven. She would love to have a heart that is pure. A heart without envy...to not always want for more. To not give in to the impulse of gossip. To not judge someone. She admits to being anxious to see what that's going to be like. When Ashley was dying, she got close to that state of purity Barb aspires to. One day in her hospital room, her friends were gossiping and being catty about something. Ashley seemed to be sleeping, but suddenly she raised her finger and shook it at her friends and simply said, "No gossip girls". After that Barb tried to be more conscientious about it...but "dang it's hard"...and in her own assessment, she's usually not successful.

Though a definite believer in Heaven, Barb is hesitant to say that she believes in hell. From her upbringing and traditional Catholic beliefs, she grew up believing you have to accept God as your savior in order to get to heaven. But that doesn't necessarily mean there's a devil. She thinks the devil is this life...that we're living the devil right now. She's struggled with that question internally because she's known people who committed suicide and was always told as a kid that that's a mortal sin...because you took a life. And yet, she could murder someone and accept God as her savior and be forgiven. If you commit suicide, you don't have that opportunity. One of her sister Kelsey's friends in high school took his life. Barb couldn't bring herself to believe that he could go to hell for that because he suffered from depression, especially because he believed in God.

That's what brought her peace with Ashley. She knew. She didn't have to worry about whether she was going to heaven. All her life she'd told her kids they're going to heaven if they believe in God and in the early days of mourning Ashley's death, she didn't even know if she believed there's a heaven. She was really forced to think about that for herself in a very real way…not just as a concept. It wasn't long before her faith and the comfort it brought her returned.

We all have an image of what heaven will be like… based on theology, The Bible, what we need it to be, or even stories we read about people who have had a near-death experience. Barb imagines our bodies are restored to perfection. For her this means Ashley doesn't have the tumors in her eye and neck, so her face is no longer misshapen. She imagines her dad can see again. All of our physical ailments are gone. These thoughts are more and more prevalent in her mind because she's now older than her dad was when he died. Kelsey is the age her sister was when she was taken and will certainly outlive her by many years.

THE HAPPY PLACE

Barb's life in heaven will be spent in fellowship with friends and family, time for worship and praise (after all that's why we're there). She'll just enjoy her days... the weather always sunny, visiting in beautiful settings...and most importantly Jesus speaking in regular settings like He did when He was on earth. As she gets older, she has fewer questions. It's a belief and understanding she has that have carried her through the worst time in her life. And once she gets to heaven, there will be no more questions.

Ashley was in hospice care the last few days of her life, and Barb now volunteers at that hospice house. When she tells residents what brought her there, they look at her in amazement and confusion...but they'll ask her to tell them about Ashley and what her last days and hours were like. Because of her experience and her deep faith, she's able to provide comfort to those who are nearing the end of their lives on earth. Surprisingly, Barb says it's very comforting there, calling it "as homey as you can make it." The nurses are so special. They don't try to sugarcoat anything...everybody knows why they're there. It's not that anyone is coming there to get better because the only medication is for pain and to alleviate suffering. If you want to talk to a chaplain, they bring one in. They're very accommodating to "what do you need?" "what do you want?" "what can we do for you?" And they stay away if you need them to stay away. Care is unique to each person. Most, if not all, of them believe in heaven.

When Barb talks to people who are in hospice care, they don't need her to answer any questions for them. She's just making sure that what they're thinking and feeling is all right. Being able to be honest and empathic allows her to validate them. With some you can see the worry, others you can see the relief. She can't recall ever having a conversation with anybody specifically about what's next. They all know the end is coming for them, and the freedom from pain and illness is comforting.

As you might expect, asking a mom to relive the loss of her beloved daughter can be overwhelming and heavy. In order to lighten the mood a bit, I asked her what she'd want to eat in Heaven and why...prompted by the story on which this book is based. What it wouldn't be is ketchup bread (she's grinning at the childhood memory). She thinks it would be crab legs because when she's eating crab, she feels like she's in Heaven on earth.

Barb Abernethy has survived something no parent should have to experience. Not only has she not succumbed to her grief, she has brought something good out of her loss. In Ashley's memory, Barb established Ashley Abernethy's Purple Star Foundation, dedicated to finding a cure for SNUC (Sinonasal Undifferentiated Carcinoma)...dedicated to finding a cure. At the time of Ashley's diagnosis, research on SNUC was virtually nonexistent. To date they have raised almost $150,000 through her personal fund-raising efforts, and she has partnered with two organizations to work exclusively on research for SNUC. Barb says it's what Ashley would have done. And while this initiative is noble and tremendously valuable, I believe it is Barb's faith and testimony that carry on Ashley's memory in the most profound way.

Barb was with Ashley when she took her first breath, and while she wishes to the end of the world that Ashley was still here, she was also blessed to be with her when she took her last. Providing comfort to her in the midst of the storm is the resounding faith that they will one day be together again...and they'll never be anything but happy.

KEEP YOUR FORK

Recipe for Happiness

<u>Ingredients</u>
2 heaping cups of patience
1 heart, full of love
2 handfuls of generosity
plenty of faith
1 handful of understanding
dash of laughter
generous sprinkle of kindness

<u>Directions</u>
- Combine patience, love and generosity with understanding.
- Add a dash of laughter and sprinkle generously with kindness.
- Add plenty of faith and mix well.
- Spread over a period of a lifetime. *Serve everyone you meet.*

Tattoo on Your Heart

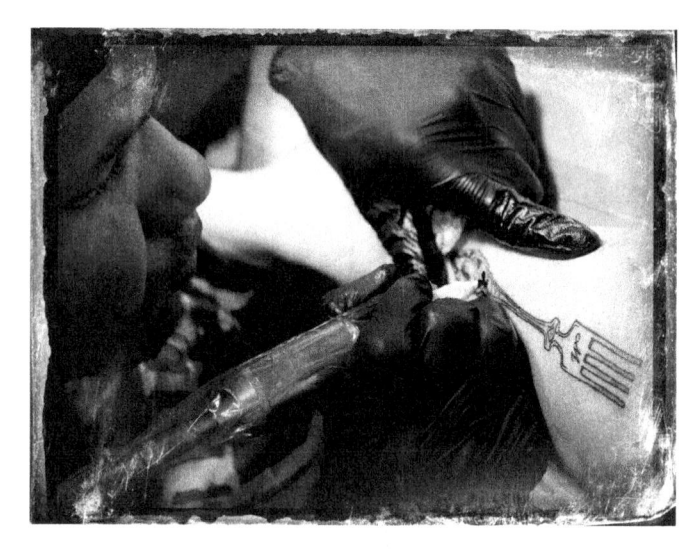

*But the Lord is with me as a mighty, fearsome one;
therefore my persecutors shall stumble,
and they shall not prevail.
They shall be greatly ashamed, for they shall not prosper;
their everlasting confusion shall never be forgotten.*
—Jeremiah 20:11

Shawn Newbins is a biracial stunt-bike-riding Christian tattoo artist with only one leg. At first take, it would not be difficult to make assumptions about who he is. If you chose to be so narrow-minded, you would miss out on getting to know an amazing...and complicated...man.

Shawn's parents met in the early 70's. His father was a cocaine and heroin dealer who was indicted for federal drug trafficking and ran with his pregnant wife to Canada. Less than two months after Shawn's birth, the FBI kicked in their door and extradited his father back to a Colorado federal prison to start a ten-year sentence. Shawn never knew his father...only through stories of a narcissistic controlling man who got his wife involved in a life she never wanted...walking a path for which she was ill-prepared. Ahh...the things we do for love.

Shawn was raised by his single mom who was well-educated from a good family led by a strong husband and father. From all appearances, he had a typical Midwestern childhood. He was an active kid, involved in peewee baseball, football, basketball, judo, etc. He admits to being easily influenced into all kinds of mischief, but he always knew the difference between right and wrong. Raising a child on her own was challenging, and Shawn got used to "running over" his mother and doing whatever he pleased...

KEEP YOUR FORK

or throwing a fit until he got was he wanted. With the help of her father, she did the best she could. Shawn was an ornery kid, always into something. He'd use a rope to sneak out of his bedroom window to play with the neighborhood kids. Like many kids who grew up in the 80's, he became obsessed with skateboarding… even built a half pipe in his backyard.

As he approached adolescence, Shawn decided he was all grown up and could hang in the streets with his skater friends. This led to him eventually being sent to live in a group home after getting caught shoplifting. Graduating from the group home to a detention center where he stayed for about a year, he was introduced to gangs and racism. He can only imagine the heartbreaking devastation for his mother to see him go down the same path as his father. Shawn was released to his mother at the age of 16; and in spite of what he'd already been through, he believes this is when his problems really started.

> *"As many of us who have been incarcerated before feel upon release we must catch up on everything we missed out on. Or we have a reputation to uphold and people expect us to act the same as we were before. he was just a spoiled brat who now could do what he wanted and try to live up to the standards which where learned while incarcerated because*

let's be honest, jail is like college. You either go there to learn all you can about how not to get caught next time or you go in there and transform into something you're not. Very few use it to better themselves mentally."

Shawn's grandfather was the only father figure he had, and he learned a lot from him. Like his grandfather, he developed a love of meeting new people and calls himself "a people person." As a child he was told he should consider a career as a lawyer or a priest because of his desire to help others. He has been told by five priests from five different states that he should be a leader in the church. But he's always run from that because he sees himself as a sinner and a complete failure in life. He would let it go in one ear and out the other because he thought to do this he must stop chasing the world and become a saint. And to him that sounded boring and wrong...and an impossible dream. He's always glorified what he saw on TV, movies and street legends...and he thought that was the life he wanted and in fact was destined to lead.

In July 1994 Shawn was with a friend traveling down I-35 when another vehicle approached their car, swerving and yelling out the window. Shawn pulled out a hand gun and opened fire on them. After a brief police chase, Shawn and his buddy were arrested and charged with several felonies, including aggravated assault. That was the beginning of his adult criminal career…he is what the courts call a career criminal, having over 18 felonies on his record. He served about ten years in prison between the ages 15 and 26. He still finds it hard to cope with the fact of knowing he spent his critical learning years among troubled men, labeling it as a feeling of abandonment. But for some reason he always thought it was the life that was meant for him.

Shawn started riding motorcycles before most of us learned to drive, starting out on four-wheelers. He says he used to jump four-wheelers, doing doubles and triples. He would "just launch over cars," loving the feeling of almost flying. He is in fact a self-proclaimed adrenaline junkie. He got a street bike and just took off…no tags, no insurance…didn't even know how to ride it. Back then he was running the streets and doing tattoos at a time when there wasn't a tattoo shop in every strip mall, mixed in with the nail salons and phone stores. Without any training, he had discovered a natural talent for body art and started what he calls tattoo parties where people get together to get tattoos. He was making money every day and living a life he loved but had never dreamed he'd have…a life he never believed he deserved.

On May 17, 2008 Shawn was at home resting before one of his late-night tattoo parties when he decided

TATTOO ON YOUR HEART

to have lunch and ride with a buddy. Somewhere between lunch and their destination, he was hit from behind by another bike. Witnesses say they were traveling at speeds over 140 miles per hour. He was thrown to the concrete, sliding down the highway upside down. When he stopped sliding, he could hear a ringing sound in his ears and everything seemed to be at a standstill. He tried to stand up but fell back down and tried to scoot off the highway to the shoulder. He looked at his feet and saw a shiny white object poking out of his torn jeans. He instantly knew he had broken his leg and recalls overhearing his buddy on the phone telling someone he didn't think Shawn was going to make it. He lost a lot of blood. All he could think was, "Is this it?" His selfishness has once again hurt the ones he loved and himself. He started saying the Lord's Prayer and preparing for his death. But what came next he could never imagine.

He knows without a doubt that God was with him. The EMTs were there in seconds and he was at the hospital within 45 minutes. He remembers lying on the side of the road holding the hand of a witness and telling the EMT his name, age and contact info. He tried to keep his composure. He didn't cry until they were setting his leg to move him. That is when the burning started. It felt like his leg was on fire and the paramedics wouldn't give him any pain relief until he'd been seen by a doctor. Finally settled in the emergency room, he got a morphine shot and was told they were going to fix him up…'don't worry.' He woke up in ICU missing his right leg below the knee.

He went through extensive physical therapy and rode an emotional rollercoaster that was far more challenging than one of his rides on a crotch rocket. People from all over Johnson County and Kansas City came to support him in his time of need. He always wondered if anyone would care if he died… *"Would anyone come to my funeral?"* His eyes and his heart were now opened to the love of those whose lives he had touched. But this was only the beginning of his problems.

His girlfriend at the time had his phone while he was in the hospital and found out that Shawn was involved in several affairs. He had never respected women; he would tell them what they wanted to hear in order to get sex. He had a serious sex addiction and was chasing the fame and fortune of a single tattoo artist on the rise.

"I was addicted to the world."

He had a great woman at home and couldn't see it because of his selfishness and allegiance to the streets and the world. He had a reputation in Kansas City as a great tattoo artist and a womanizer. Her family and friends hated him behind his back but always smiled to his face. They were trying to protect her from what they knew wasn't right for her or her son. But somehow they stayed together and she turned her back on her family and chose him. He couldn't see that, and had now lost her. He wishes more than anything that he could go back to how it was before, but he can't and now he must suffer the consequences. He prays that one day he can show her he's sorry and won't take advantage of her again.

Shawn believes God has your life planned out for you, and you can stay on the right track…His track…and have somewhat of a meaningful life…whatever that meaning is. He believes everything is tied together, even with death. People die for a reason, even if that reason may not be revealed immediately, if ever. God meant for him to survive that devastating motorcycle crash.

When Shawn went to prison he studied different religions; he dabbled in Islam and he looked at various other faiths. He says when you're in prison, you've lost yourself somewhere along the way; and it's easy to be drawn to something that appears to be working for someone else. Raised by a mother and grandfather who were Mennonites and believed in going to church, Shawn was not unfamiliar with God and faith. While not always front of mind, it certainly was part of his character.

KEEP YOUR FORK

*"Train up a child in the way he should go:
and when he is old, he will not depart from it."
—Proverbs 22:6*

But Shawn knows this Bible verse is not always the case. Sometimes a child is going to screw up and make choices that have nothing to do with how he was raised. No matter how you raise them up, people go out and try to find their way in the world.

Understanding that changes the game completely. He's now a father himself and is careful of what he says to his kids and is aware that he's an example for them of what it means to be a Christian man. He knows they believe in God. When they're together, they eat as a family and they pray together. He wants them to understand what family means.

For a long time he wanted to quit tattooing because he felt that it was wrong. He thought for a time that he wanted to do a Christian tattoo shop where he would have a chance to minister to people while he's tattooing. But as a Dalmatian has spots so we can easily identify them from other dogs, Shawn believes he doesn't have to say his is a Christian tattoo shop in order to distinguish himself from other artists. People are going to know who he is and they're going to come to him and respect him enough not to bring things to him that are not of God. If the sign over his shop says "Christian," he would be limiting himself to one type of client, and it might cause some to avoid him. Jesus wanted to hang out with all sinners, all day long. He was a man comfortable with street people, and that's who Shawn spends his time with as well. He has a chance to minister to people who might never otherwise hear the Word. One thing he's promised God is that he won't tattoo skulls...he doesn't want to do anything that is pro-death.

His walk with Christ has been on a road full of ruts and detours, yet his attitude and outlook remain positive. The days of waking up without any pain are dead and gone. His leg feels like it's in a vise about 70% of the day. There are days when he can get up and just walk off like nothing happened; then there are days when it's so swollen just getting the prosthetic leg on is a great task. He uses crutches most of each day.

The emotional healing is probably the worst part about the injury; to wonder why he was spared is never far from front of mind. He's seen death in front of him on more than one occasion so he's not scared to die. He's scared of what comes next and what becomes of his family after. To leave them behind without anything but bad memories of him and financial devastation is constantly on his mind.

KEEP YOUR FORK

Physically he can do anything, but mentally he gets stuck sometimes thinking that he can't do certain things due to his accident. But that is not the case. He refuses to use his leg as a crutch as to why he wants to quit because people are constantly watching him to see if he's going to break down and quit. But to see the faces of those who are watching him when they see he's unbreakable is worth it to him. He will never give up on what he believes in…and that is God, and his family.

Shawn Newbins shines the light of Christ as a perfect example of what God wants us to be. It's easy when you see someone who's never had to struggle to say, "He loves God. Everything's all good." Not to say that their walk with Christ is not as strong, but when you've had to struggle with anything, any diversity, any kind of challenge, you have to face things that other people won't; and walking with Christ is not always the easiest path to take.

He's been fortunate enough that he has always believed in an afterlife. But he doesn't really think about it much. He doesn't know what heaven is going to look like. Many of us have an image of a pearly gate, but not Shawn. Instead, he thinks God is choosing his angels right now for his heaven war; and the devil is choosing his angels for his war. When you die, if you're on God's side you're going to have your sword and wings and get to do battle. After this world there's another world that has to have his battle. He hopes he gets his wings…he wants to hit the demon in the head with something.

Shawn is constantly at war with himself feuding between good and evil, right and wrong and heaven or hell. He sits in sorrow for himself and admits to an occasional suicidal thought because he doesn't understand why he survived when so many before him have not from traumatic accidents like his. Life is a constant chess game in which you must make sure that all your moves are protected by another move before it so you don't lose. He's been knocked down and stood upon for a long time. But never has God left his side. He continues to stunt his motorcycle and produce and film bike videos. He can do everything he used to do except run…and he probably could do that with a little effort. He used to think his pastor was the most blessed man he knows, but he thinks he was wrong all those years. He is the most blessed person he knows because he succeeds in anything he touches or tries to do. He's never had any training in his tattoo profession yet feeds a total of nine families through his business success.

It would have been easy for Shawn to live down to life's expectations, but he chose another path. He's no saint, but he is on his way to heaven now "instead of down below." He is pursuing a life of motivational speaking and stunting and raising his son and daughter better than the streets raised him. It just goes to show it doesn't matter where you come from, trouble is around every corner. But to have someone to look up to as mentor or positive role model is a must. He believes through this he can steer his family in the right direction away from the paths he has taken to get where he is today.

He prays the prayer, "Lord, thank you. Whatever happens now, it's Your will." If you believe that, that's how you have to live; you have to believe it.

Father with a Capital F

*Furthermore we have had fathers of our flesh
who corrected us, and we gave them reverence.
Shall we not far rather be in subjection
unto the Father of Spirits, and live?*
—*Hebrews 12:9*

FATHER WITH A CAPITAL F

Mitch Gold is a brilliant man...the Ph.D. behind his name is only one indication. He is well steeped in his Jewish faith, and extremely involved in the local Jewish community. It seems impossible to mention a name in Kansas City without Mitch telling you he knows them from the Jewish Community Center. As someone who grew up Catholic—taught that Jews didn't believe in a definitive heaven—I found myself curious as to his perspective on Heaven.

Until recently he was skeptical about the whole idea of the afterlife. Trained as a scientist, it's hard for him to get his head around the concept of an unexplainable life after the one we know here on earth. Life is life, death is death. But that's how his parents grew up as well...as scientists. His mom is a very intelligent, wise, hearty woman who in her late seventies remains very sharp. A couple of weeks after his dad passed away, his mom told him this story where she was in bed and having trouble getting to sleep. She felt something, literally felt an arm around her...and she just knew it was her husband. Coming from his mom, that meant something, and it opened his mind. On a daily basis, he now thinks about what his dad would think of what he's doing right now, the decisions he's making, how he treats people. His dad has become his compass.

Mitch was raised in a conservative synagogue, although his father wasn't particularly religious. His father would show up the required 2-3 times a year during the high holidays, but Mitch went frequently with his mom, especially in his teenage years. They'd make a day of it, go to breakfast beforehand on a Saturday and then go to synagogue together. While not particularly religious, Mitch's dad was his greatest influence growing up. From him, Mitch got all the threads that make him Mitch…intelligence, empathy, humor and kindness. Like many parents, he didn't realize fully how strong his dad was and how important he was in his life until he had children of his own. Being a parent has put a mirror in front of him, the mirror that is his father. He now understands the hopes, fears and flaws in himself as an adult…things that he knows his dad realized in himself but didn't want to expose to Mitch to allow him to figure out for himself.

Mitch's wife was raised in a more traditional, orthodox culture and today they raise their kids in a fairly conservative Jewish environment. The key for them is actually less about where you are on the conservative spectrum and more about that they role model for the kids. He doesn't care if somebody is reformed or conservative. At the end of the day, he and his wife are trying to live these values and they have to role model even the most basic behaviors…going to synagogue, lighting candles on Friday night, all of those things they believe you have to role model for their kids if they expect them to carry on their religion.

FATHER WITH A CAPITAL F

Mitch speaks of different types of Jews... traditional, reformed, conservative...and I asked him to explain the difference. A traditional/conservative Jew might follow the most basic description of observing the Sabbath which means from sundown on Friday to sundown on Saturday, you do not drive a car, use electricity, nothing with an on/off switch, essentially devolving to the most basic existence...casting off all conveniences and getting as close to God in prayer as you can. This means if you go to synagogue, you're going to walk there. You might see the more orthodox people dressed in black, walking to synagogue. In a more orthodox synagogue, If you're a woman, you sit on one side of the synagogue. There's a glass divider, and men sit on the other side. While the whole service is going on, men and women are not supposed to be sitting together in traditional orthodox. Mitch speaks of a more orthodox synagogue in the local area. It is actually one of the more fun the area because despite the fact they practice separation of the genders, they like to have quite a bit of fun during their service. There's dancing while you're praying.

You compare that to a more reformed temple, where there is less Hebrew and more English in the service. It's a much calmer, tepid environment where people don't get up and get as passionate. Despite the fact you can be reformed and the service less traditional, it doesn't necessarily mean there's more passion or more excitement in one over the other. During their services, whether it's through prayer, Hebrew prayer or English readings, there are dozens of references to doing the right thing. People who do the right thing forgive each other, just as God forgives everything if the person is honest and willing to change.

God made man in His image. So there are probably some of the same frailties and weaknesses in God that are in man, given that we were made in His image. To some extent, God is somewhat of a person.

Jews believe in the Torah and in the Old Testament. When you start looking at books like Genesis and Exodus, Leviticus, Numbers, Deuteronomy, that's the foundation of Jewish beliefs. In the really reformed temples, they may not even pull out the Torah, but at synagogues there will be a weekly reading and you'll see a number of people going up and reading passages, chanting passages in Hebrew from the Torah. Those readings span those five books and beyond and take the better part of the year to get through. A good portion of the book of Exodus talks about the 40 years that the Jews spent wandering in the desert when they left Egypt. They spend a good part of their services delving into that. Mitch's sons went to a Jewish day school up until about 7th grade and the running joke was you'd ask them at dinner what they learned that day. They'd say, "We talked again about the Jews wandering through the desert. How long do they do that? Seems like that's all they did."

Readings talk about the shift when they left Egypt, this was a huge band of people wandering who had no code. They were praying to idols they built. Indulging in activities that are frowned upon these days. There was no code, no binding effort here and that's where you start getting into the story of Moses going up on to the mountain and seeing the burning bush and revealing the 10 Commandments and bringing those back down to the people saying look, he has seen God. This is what we now live by. That's what we spend a good part of our time reading through the Torah talking about that.

The lights have really come on for Mitch in the last several months because of the loss of his dad. He finds himself thinking less about God and more about his dad. He really believes that his dad is in a wonderful place right now and that he's watching. Mitch feels as though his father monitors his actions and so Mitch wonders what his dad would think. What would his dad do? What would he think of him making the decisions Mitch is making? He uses that as a benchmark for everything from how he approaches his work to how he talks to his kids to how he treats his wife Lori. He uses that as a benchmark because for him, his dad was the benchmark. It wasn't anything written in the

Torah or written in a prayer book. The benchmark was what he observed and what he admired in his father. Even though he wasn't what he'd call an observant Jew, he was a great man in that he was wise and he had an impeccable code that he lived by; a code of integrity and honesty and kindness. He was a fair man, and he made people hold their feet to the fire. And when there was something someone said that he didn't agree with, he would debate it to the end. But he did so in a way that was kind. That's what guides Mitch Gold.

While it remains unclear if there is a place called heaven, Mitch believes when people have lived the Commandments and the life that God has dictated to us, they'll be judged and rewarded with some kind of afterlife. There will be unification with God and with loved ones who have passed. His personal belief is that it's somewhat of a collective where we are not really ourselves in the afterlife but that we are rather bits and pieces of loved ones and God as well. A place where the souls of loved ones are intertwined into a collective of love, warmth and understanding without words. Where this collection of souls is floating without boundaries but with purpose. That belief may vary a little bit when you start talking to people who are traditional Jews vs. Reformed Jews vs. Conservative Jews; but all in all he says "we're driven by a belief that if you do good things and you follow the code, you're going to be rewarded when you're gone." He imagines there being endless time with no pressure to end conversations or hugs.

In some religions, it seems as if the afterlife is used as a threat or a manipulation in order to assure compliance. Mitch doesn't see an afterlife as a punishment; he doesn't believe there is a hell. That said, people of the Jewish faith do believe that God will judge everyone in some way. If you look in the Torah and at the Old Testament, God is not necessarily a kind God. Sodom and Gomorrah for instance. He has smote down populations of people that didn't get on board with the program. Mitch doesn't see the afterlife being held out as a reward; he sees it as an additional motivator, an additional carrot of sorts, that hopefully reinforces what people already believe and know about being good people. It's a reminder from God to keep doing great things right because this is all leading toward *something*. It's a beacon for those who lose their way, get tired or lazy, forget the direction they're headed.

He doesn't know if heaven is a place in terms of how they think of as a place. It's essentially beyond our understanding. It's a place that may be a place in our mind, or it may be part of a collective where that part of our mind goes with other people's pieces of their minds. He doesn't know.

KEEP YOUR FORK

For those who have not done such a great job here, Mitch considers a couple of possibilities. One is when you die, you die. And that's it. Everything is shut off, you're done. Another possibility may be getting another chance to do it over again. And whether that looks like reincarnation or what have you, you're going to do this again until you are vested and ready for heaven. Think about it from a parental standpoint, with God as parent, where essentially He is trying to teach a lesson. Some people will learn that lesson quickly through wisdom, insight and what they learn along the way. Others may take a couple of times to learn that lesson. He wants to believe that this is a proving ground. Somebody is watching, evaluating our actions. Back to how God made us with all our frailties and weaknesses, this is a set of experiences. We're going to make mistakes, but how we react and learn from those mistakes is what matters. God's plan is for us to continually improve and become better… we're essentially proving ourselves for whatever that afterlife is.

Mitch Gold is a man of great faith, influenced and driven by both his Heavenly Father and his earthly father. When he gets to Heaven, it's no surprise that the first person he wants to see is his dad. And when he sees his dad again, he would say, "Dad, I know."

The Witch

People only see what they are prepared to see.
—Ralph Waldo Emerson

Pagan

noun pa·gan \ pā-gən\
1. one who has little or no religion and who delights in sensual pleasures and material goods: an irreligious or hedonistic person

Do not turn to mediums or necromancers; do not seek them out, and so make yourselves unclean by them: I am the Lord your God. (Leviticus 19:31)

Of all the interviews we did for this book, the conversation with Rev. Shae Moyers was the most surprising. I went into our session with some preconceived notions of paganism depicted in the Webster's Dictionary definition and Bible verse above…someone who is non-religious, self-gratifying and certainly not Christian. Shae Moyers not only dispelled my myths but revealed herself to be one of the more spiritual beings I've had the pleasure of meeting.

From a Christian viewpoint, pagans are generally characterized as those who are caught up in any religious ceremony, act or practice that is not distinctly Christian. Correspondingly, Jews and Muslims also use the term *pagans* to describe those outside their religion. Others define the term *paganism* as any religion outside of Buddhism, Hinduism, Judaism and Christianity; whereas some argue that a pagan is anyone with no religion at all.

KEEP YOUR FORK

Rudimentary internet research reveals that a pagan is considered to be one who, for the most part, has no religion and indulges in worldly delights and material possessions; someone who revels in sensual pleasures; a hedonistic or self-indulgent individual. Another, more modern term is *neo-paganism*, which refers to some of the contemporary forms of paganism such as Wicca.

Shae Moyers is a self-described clairvoyant intuitive and medium with over twenty-seven years' experience with the gift of insight and ability to communicate with those who have crossed over. She provides her clients with "personalized soul-healing experiences" and is known for her amazing accuracy and ability to clearly "see" to the heart of the matter. She is warm and welcoming, comfortable in her own skin. The woman who answered the door to us is short in stature and long on energy. She has a buzz cut tipped in what mostly closely resembles raspberry. She is at once your sister, your best friend and a trusted confidant. Being in her presence is powerful…and comforting. She is clear in her beliefs and her purpose and at times refers to herself as a witch, a medium and a priestess.

Officially, Shae is an ordained minister and spiritual counselor and has five ministerial ordinations. She is educated in many religions and well respected in both the new thought and the pagan communities.

THE WITCH

Unofficially she admits to being a witch, and she wears the badge proudly.

Shae was born into a family of both fundamentalist Christian and Catholic backgrounds. Her mother and father separated when she was six months old, when her mother packed the car and moved back to St. Louis from San Diego. She was a single mom, working and going to school and felt she wouldn't be able to give Shae the attention she needed, so Shae went to live with her great-grandmother...a spirited woman who was about 4'11" and who on Sunday mornings stood on a stove, cranked the radio up and sang old-time gospel hymns. Her mother was certainly part of her life but was not her primary caregiver during those early years. Shae inherited her gift from her great-grandmother; she was the one who taught Shae it was acceptable and nothing to be ashamed of.

Shae says, "I knew I was different at about 2 years of age. I saw stuff." She recalled going to the cemetery to visit the grave of her great-grandfather. They were close...Shae was the first great-great grandchild, and he spoiled her rotten. She was having a conversation with him there at the gravesite as if he were physically present. When they were ready to leave, Shae began crying and wouldn't get in the car. She told them Opa, as she called her great-great grandfather, was coming with them. They hadn't realized her conversation was actually a dialog. That was when they got an inkling of what was going on.

Shae recalled the first visitation she received when she was about 8 years old.

> *"My great-grandfather who I never met passed away when my mother was 15. When we visited his widow, my great-grandmother, I would sleep in her bed. I woke up one night and saw this man with a dark suit and glasses sitting on the edge of the bed and he's petting her. I hid under the covers and wouldn't come back out. He was there for two nights in a row. I asked my grandmother, 'did you see that man? There was a man in the bedroom.' Remember the old obituary cards you'd get with the black and white photo? She had his on her dresser. She also had a picture of them maybe a year or so before he was killed. He was killed in a car accident in front of their house. So he literally died in front of the house where this event happened. I said "that's him!" and pointed to the obituary card. She said, 'are you sure?' and I said, 'grandma that's him.' And then I read it and realized he's dead. She looked it, petted the picture and said, 'I guess she sees you Luther. I'm okay, thanks for checking.'"*

THE WITCH

The second visitation was when she was 12 or 13. Her step-great-grandmother was in the hospital and was not expected to live. Shae's mother was the last person she spoke to. She said, "I need some rest" and then passed away. About that time Shae started crying. She got really upset because she kept getting a flash and couldn't explain what it was. She remembers getting very cold and seeing her step-great-grandmother. She stood in the door, blew Shae a kiss, and was gone. At that moment when Shae started crying, her mother called to let her know her grandmother had passed.

It wasn't until her late teens, however, that Shae began to explore her abilities. Her mother had a psychic party at her house, and Miss Esther (who mentored Sylvia Brown) came in. When Shae arrived, she stopped everything and looked at Shae's grandmother, looked at Shae and said, "I was waiting for you to get here, where have you been? Child, you know you have this. You'll come see me when you're ready." And six months later she did. At that point Shae began doing readings for friends. That was where it started.

Shae's purpose in life is quite simple, in spite of the complexity of her gift and how it manifests itself. She wants people to remember who they are, to feel whole and to feel holy. She believes a priestess is a vessel, in service to the Divine…and that means helping people remember who they are.

> *"I made a choice. I always wanted to be of service. You give back to the community. If you have more, you give back to others who don't. My goal is to fan your spark. If I help you remember who you are or help you heal or help you make a difference, then I've done my job. This work for me is very sacred. I take it very seriously. My job is to be a bridge between the mundane world and the spiritual world. I walk in both worlds."*

Shae has a natural curiosity and has studied extensively world religions, Wicca and the occult. She is fascinated with nature, and having grown up in the country it was a natural progression to explore astrology, then Eastern philosophy. As a reader and an intuitive, Shae is like a confessional. People come to her more readily than they'll talk to a therapist. She wanted to be armed for those conversations, so she went to ministerial school. She carries the title reverend proudly and wants people to know that she didn't just click a couple of icons online…she studied, read and learned. She wants to be viewed as a teacher.

"We all look for God because we're wounded. There's something in us that's broken that we want to heal. So when people ask me about the priestess thing, priestess is an easier answer than saying I was mad because I wanted to be a priest, but women can't be Catholic priests; and being a nun didn't appeal to me. Nuns are lay people, lay clergy. If I can make people less afraid, I've accomplished something."

Shae's spirituality is the result of her gift. She was always fascinated with history and was in fact a history major in college. She loved reading about saints and mystics and remembers a conversation with her childhood priest. Shae had grown up Catholic…got married in the Catholic Church, taught CCD, her family helped found one of the oldest Catholic churches in Olathe, KS. But at 28 she found herself struggling with her faith, and that created a good deal of guilt. She had a strong belief in God and knew how He provided her with her foundation.

> *"If it hadn't been for God I would have killed myself after my father passed away. I was a daddy's girl. Even though I wasn't his blood child he raised me and there's no way I could have gotten through it without God. God is everywhere and God is nowhere, but you have to have faith in something."*

But Catholicism wasn't providing her with the spiritual support she needed, so she went to her childhood priest to resign from teaching CCD, and to tell him she was going to seminary. She cried. This is a man who had confirmed her, who had led her through marriage encounter counseling and officiated the wedding with her husband. And in this moment of spiritual crisis, he didn't let her down. He told her he knew that she sees spirits and those who had passed on but that all the great mystics have. He didn't care what faith she pursued, as long as she believed in something. He knows that she treats her gift it with the sacredness it deserves. That gift is why Shae was put here. It's why she has such a deep faith.

Identifying herself as Pagan means she doesn't worship a bearded man in the sky. People who identify themselves as pagan believe that Spirit is in everything, and everything is holy. It doesn't matter what you look like or who you love. Even a mass murderer has a spark of the Divine. Normal religion teaches that God is external so we are always looking for God outside ourselves when really God is within each of us. If you want to get into a contextual label of pagan, that's it: they identify themselves as Divine. Sometimes God is masculine, sometimes God is feminine. It depends on the situation. Shae prays every morning. She prays every night. The only time she doesn't approve of religion as a whole is when it makes people sad or when it debases or diminishes their humanness.

Shae has Catholic friends, and you can imagine that they get into philosophical debates. But they have the same God…it's their approach that's different. In the

THE WITCH

pagan community Shae is a vocal rebel, refusing to be labeled even in the community where she's placed herself. She says she is a priestess but is also known in Kansas City as "a witch", and she doesn't mind a bit. Witch or priestess…for Shae it's one and the same. Witch is a title, and it means a wise woman, an elder of the tribe, an old crone. It's acknowledgment of a woman's value and while for most of us the term 'witch' doesn't have a good connotation, clearly Shae wears the label proudly.

Shae always believed in an afterlife. Why would God take people away if He wasn't going to bring them back in some fashion? Because of her gift, it's very comforting to know that if she's in trouble, she can get answers from those who have passed on. It's a blessing and a curse…she can't turn it off. The Catholic Church teaches purgatory and flames, but Shae wasn't taught that. She was taught a loving God who looks after everyone: gay, straight, whatever. That's the God she grew up knowing. While deeply spiritual with a strong faith, she doesn't identify with any specific religion. She is often asked if she believes in God. That question elicits a resounding, "Absolutely!"

All she does is talk about afterlife with people, and she calls it "a sacred trust." Clients will often come with a desire to connect with a particular person who has crossed over, and sometimes that connection will be made. It depends on how strong the spirit is. Sometimes it's one person or they come in looking for one person and that's not the person that shows up. It's not as if they've crossed over and are not coming back. They come back to check on us. It's an elevated state of consciousness. They're still here, just in a different form; and they're forced to communicate at a higher frequency, at a more subtle level. If they want you to know something, they do something to get your attention.

> *"My house sometimes is like Grand Central Station."*

Shae has a better relationship with her dad now than when he was alive. She understands more. Those who have crossed over want you to remember them when they were at their best. They pray for you all the time. We wonder whether they're okay… that's the number one question Shae is asked by her clients. Our loved ones want us to know they're safe. They want to reassure us that they're okay. The greatest gift Shae gives her clients is closure or comfort or validation.

The help is there if we ask for it, but it may not be in the form we expect or desire.

> *"I'm going through a career change, returning to corporate after having had my own*

THE WITCH

consulting firm. I asked daddy, "What would you do?" I ran into his best friend (we called him Uncle Mike when we were growing up) the other day and he said he heard I was looking for a job. He told me my dad would be really proud of me. My dad was never into all this psychic stuff. Called it hocus pocus. But I believe they channel through other people. They send people to you. I was really, really low...having a bad day. Figuring I had ruined my career, never going to get the job I want, professional suicide. But Uncle Mike said, "You might not have taken the path he would have taken, but you're carrying on his legacy. Your dad would kill you if you quit. He didn't raise you like that. You're a success in your own way and your own right and that's your legacy. He physically dropped the ball; you're still here to run with it. What are you going to do with it?" It didn't hit me until I left...it was a 10-minute conversation at QuikTrip...I just had my ass kicked by my dad."

Spirits who have crossed over want to be treated with respect and acknowledged; we all want to be seen and heard. We want to know we made a difference. They're not lacking emotion; they miss us just as we miss them. Sometimes they will use other people to come through. Shae gets images or dates. It's not as if she sees someone in her living room in a casket. Spirits will sometimes use correlations from her own life to help make the connection. Or they'll show her something. She has to repeat it exactly as she hears or sees it, and she does her best to describe it exactly. Shae always tells people to open themselves up to this. Listen. But don't listen with your ears; listen with your heart and listen with your mind. Your heart doesn't know how to lie.

People who were not so great in this lifetime may not be so great on the other side either. Shae is a firm believer in karma. We make soul agreements when we come into this lifetime. There are stories more often now of children having past-life memories. If Shae goes into a house and they have paranormal activity, it's because the spirits are curious from the other side about what we do. *"They can't stop us from being idiots, but they can let us know they're here."*

Shae absolutely believes in reincarnation. She believes there is a reckoning that occurs; and if we don't get it right this time, we'll come back until we get it right. It could be hundreds of years, it depends on the soul. We look back on our book of life and have to reconcile our actions. It's an individual thing. We don't come back immediately but instead there's a transitional period. Shae knows that from what she has been shown and what she has been told by those

THE WITCH

who have visited from the other side. We all have to do an inventory, an assessment of what we didn't accomplish in our time on earth. There are some people who go and don't come back. They may choose to take a different role. It's a multi-dimensional thing.

Look at Pope Francis. He is busting the norm and exposing secrets; he's not governed by doctrine. He's seen the next generation and acknowledges the need for religion/spirituality to grow. He doesn't care if it's Catholic or not. He just knows that we need some type of faith in our world, and he's willing to be one of the trailblazers. People have suggested he is the reincarnation of St. Francis of Assisi.

Though Shae has ample opportunity to connect with her loved ones who have passed on, she's human. She misses her family and looks forward to the point when the veils that separate her from them will be removed. That spiritual person in her gets the connection she has now, and she realizes she's blessed to connect so intimately with her loved ones who have crossed over; but she still wants the physical connection again. She says she is afraid of dying, but not what happens after.

We all start out at the same place, and we all go back to the same place. Shae Moyers is confident in her purpose on earth. Spirits help her do her work...she provides comfort for those who remain after someone has transitioned from this earthly plane to the next. And she is clear in her beliefs. She is truly one of the most spiritual people I've met, but I would be remiss if I tried to put her into a box with a label on it. Even pagan doesn't begin to describe the depth of her connection to God and the afterlife. She says, "Don't ever walk away from what you know to be true for yourself and what you believe." And she truly walks that talk.

Midnight Goddess

Ingredients
1 1/2 oz. Vodka
2 oz. Pineapple Juice
1/2 oz. Blue Curacao
Champagne

Directions
- Place the vodka, blue curacao, pineapple juice and ice into a cocktail shaker and shake, then strain into a champagne flute and top up with champagne.

Bridge of Hope

*Faith is the pierless bridge supporting
what we see unto the scene that we do not.*
—Emily Dickinson

BRIDGE OF HOPE

As we arrived for our scheduled interview with Rev. Adam Hamilton, he greeted us with a warm handshake and said it was perfect timing for a discussion about Heaven. He had just come from delivering the eulogy at the funeral of a three-year-old boy. He was right...the freshness of that experience and its accompanying oxymoronic feelings of sadness and joy, loss and hope, pain and comfort, provided a great foundation for our conversation.

When Adam Hamilton was 14, a Pentecostal evangelist knocked on his front door to invite him to church. Adam went and over time felt increasingly drawn to God. After reading the Gospel of Luke, he decided to become a Christian. Fast forward 35 years, and he now leads a congregation of over 20,000 at the largest United Methodist church in the United States.

For all that he has accomplished, growing his congregation from 4 people meeting in a funeral home to leading multiple campuses across the Greater Kansas City area, Adam Hamilton is a man of great humility. His personal beliefs, of course, are biblically-based. Each weekend, his prayer is that he will make a difference in someone's life, that his message will touch someone's heart so that they may draw closer to God. His urgent desire is that those who have little or no relationship with God will be touched by his words so that they may enter into the folds of God's loving

KEEP YOUR FORK

arms. Adam Hamilton is the bridge between where you are and where you want to be.

As a Christian pastor and leader, it should surprise no one that Adam Hamilton believes in Heaven. He freely shares that one of the main reasons he believes in the afterlife, and has great hope in it, is because Jesus believed in it and taught about it. And "He didn't just teach about it. He demonstrated it." At the end of Adam's Easter service each year, he shares the same comment: "I not only believe in it; I'm counting on it."

While Adam is counting on Heaven, he also believes that God will not force anyone to go there. All are invited, not all choose to accept the invitation. Asked if he believes in hell he said that he did and views hell in ways similar to C.S. Lewis who is reported to have said, "The doors of hell are locked from the inside."

Any discussion of Heaven and who we'll find there will typically focus on humans. But what about animals, especially pets? Adam honestly admits that he hopes all animals don't go to Heaven. He'd prefer that ticks, spiders, snakes not be there. But he is open to the possibility that animals have a place in Heaven. He reminds us that Isaiah once gave a picture of the coming Messianic age in which he states that in that age, "The wolf and the lamb will feed together, and the lion will eat straw like the ox, but dust will be the serpent's food. They will neither harm nor destroy on all my holy mountain, says the Lord." This may have been simply a metaphorical way of speaking about that future realm, but it may also point to the truth that there will be animals in Heaven.

Others have argued that animals don't have souls and thus will not be in Heaven. Of course, that depends upon how you define a soul. Adam has always felt that his pets had souls. As with their human counterparts, they have intelligence, personality and character; and they express joy, protectiveness and companionship.

I love Adam's perspective on animals in Heaven. "I think that it is possible that God raises up those animals that had special meaning in our lives, and that perhaps His resurrection of these creatures is part of the gift that God gives us in Heaven." What a beautiful way of reassuring us that even our beloved pets will be with us for eternity.

So, what is Heaven like? If we can have a clearer idea of what Heaven is like, maybe some of the fear and uncertainty we have about death can be dispelled.

The Bible is surprisingly sparse in its descriptions of Heaven. The Book of Revelation gives us a few glimpses, mostly in symbolic language not meant to be taken literally. What we do know is that Jesus describes Heaven as paradise. Paradise comes from a Persian word that referred to the "king's gardens." It was often used to describe beautiful menageries with exotic animals, water features and beautiful plants and trees. Honored guests were invited to walk the king's garden with him.

Many biblical references portray Heaven as a Garden. Adam and Eve were expelled from the Garden of Eden because they disobeyed God, and we were forbidden from ever entering the garden again. Paradise was lost to us, and we were left with a world where injustice, pain, sorrow and death are a part of life. So it would make sense that Heaven would be a garden to which we would want to return…a place of redemption and healing. Maybe if we had a clearer picture of what the afterlife was like, we would not fight so hard to avoid it. As has often been said, Everyone wants to go to Heaven, but no one wants to die.

So what is life like in that afterlife? As we envision our continued connection with those on the other side, we may question how the relationship will continue. Will we have our earthly body? Will we still be married to our spouse? Here's what Adam thinks about these questions.

We will not be married in Heaven if by that we mean an exclusive and sexual relationship. Jesus said that in heaven we will neither marry nor be given in marriage. What does this mean for those who were married when they arrive in heaven? Adam expects that he and his wife will continue to love one another and share their lives together. He goes even further to say he anticipates they will actually love one another more fully and deeply than they do today. That having been said, Adam interprets Jesus' words to mean that this marital relationship in Heaven will not be sexual or romantic and that in Heaven we will have the capacity to love *all* people the way we love our spouse. A deep love and friendship with his wife and the capacity to have deep, loving friendships with others—that is how Adam pictures marriage in Heaven.

A member of his church asked Adam if those who have passed watch over us all the time. And do they hear us talking to them? Adam's answer is that he thinks there are moments when God invites those who have passed to peer down on the events happening on earth – special moments in their loved ones lives like weddings, or the birth or baptism of a child. But he doesn't heaven would be heaven if, when we die, we spend all of our time watching what happens here on earth to our children and loved ones. There will be too much to do in heaven!

Christianity affirms something called the Communion of the Saints. The idea is that we are bound together with the believers who've gone before us. So, can we speak to our loved ones who have died? As with our loved ones watching over us, Adam doesn't believe that those who have died are waiting for us to begin speaking to them. But God *is* always listening. There are times when Adam thanks God for a deceased family member, and he asks God to speak to them and let them know he's thinking about them and still loves them. And there may be moments when God allows our loved ones to hear us. It can be therapeutic to speak to them at the grave, and it may be that these are moments where God says to our loved one in heaven, "Come here, I want you to hear this." On this Adam notes that he is merely speculating as the Bible isn't clear on this.

Do you know one of the most common images for Heaven in the Bible? It is that of a banquet or a party. Jesus spoke of the afterlife as a celebration, and He chose specifically the image of a wedding banquet. Remember, in the first century most people didn't have feasts. They were poor and struggled to make ends meet. But when there was to be a wedding, a family saved and saved and then threw a party that lasted not a couple of hours like our weddings today, but nearly a week. There was dancing and food and wine and lots of laughter and joy. These were the greatest moments of life when family gathered around to celebrate the union of two people in love. And this is precisely how Jesus described Heaven...as a wedding banquet.

Adam noted, "Take the most joyful and blessed moments of your life, and take away any of the sadness and tears, and you have a picture of what heaven may be like." Adam envisions Heaven as the most wonderful times of his life here.

> *"I think of my daughter's wedding. We had all the most important people in our lives gathered in one place. There was music, feasting, singing and dancing. I have a picture of my wife dancing with her father who has since passed away. There was such joy on both of their faces. That's how I picture heaven. Take the most beautiful and deeply meaningful moments in life, and they give us a glimpse of what heaven is like."*

Another interesting dimension to Jesus' teaching on the afterlife is that some will be greater and more rewarded there and others less so. He spoke of some being "greatest in the kingdom of heaven." He speaks of differing "rewards" in heaven. He tells his disciples to do their acts of piety in secret and that God will one day reward them openly. And He says that the first shall be last and the last shall be first.

KEEP YOUR FORK

Someone once told Adam, "With all the things you've done, you should be living in a mansion in Heaven." But Adam has just the opposite feeling. He notes that he's received recognition in this life. "If I make it to heaven, and I hope I will, I'm expecting a pup tent or a pop-up camper, but even that will be better than anything in this life!" He believes those who are prominent in Heaven will be those who quietly sacrificed, suffered and gave of themselves without recognition while walking the earth.

When asked if he thinks the deceased can return to their loved ones on earth, Adam admits that he has had people tell him that they have seen their loved one in a physical form. A grieving wife was driving in the car and looked over to see her deceased husband seated next to her in the car. Others talk of being visited by something representing that person: a butterfly was something meaningful between a mother and child, and the mother would see butterflies in unusual places where they wouldn't normally be seen; a rainbow might be meaningful to someone and that's how they feel they are visited by a loved one who has passed on. Adam has not had such an experience of being visited in physical form by someone who's passed on.

Christians believe in Christ and the hope we have for a life beyond this one, but at times they approach their

BRIDGE OF HOPE

own deaths, or those of others they love, as though they have no hope. Adam notes that much of the crisis in the healthcare industry today is due to the inordinate amount of our resources devoted to postponing death by a few days, weeks or months. He wonders if we really trusted what Jesus teaches us about death, if we'd find greater peace devote less time, resources and even unnecessary suffering trying to postpone it.

The stories of those who have had a brush with death, or who have been with loved ones who described what they were seeing as they were dying, can be a powerful witness to the truth of the afterlife and might provide some comfort and reassurance that this isn't all there is.

A woman in Adam's congregation was in the hospital with a very serious illness; she nearly died twice. On one of those occasions she felt herself slipping away, and suddenly she was somewhere else. She described the experience as follows:

I began to see everyone that I knew who had died. The crowd was standing on both sides of the entrance as far as I could see. Everyone was clapping, waving their arms, and jumping up and down...they were so glad to see me and I them...especially my parents. I cannot even describe the beauty of the river, the

> *flowers and trees beside the water...there are no words except to say that it was beyond description...beautiful, sweet, awesome... the atmosphere was so happy. And when the doctors began to bring her back she remembers wanting to cry out, "No! Please! I want to stay!" But now, she said, "I have no fear of dying."*

If we could have a preview of what is on the other side, and really trust it, we might say with Paul, "For me to live is Christ and to die is gain!"

As the leader of such a prominent congregation, Adam has had extensive experience in ministering to those who have experienced a loss. It seems every time a tragedy occurs in the Kansas City area, there is a connection to Church of the Resurrection. The funeral of the three-year-old boy on the day of our interview is sadly not an isolated situation. Adam and the congregational care team at the Church of the Resurrection regularly visit and pray with the dying, to comfort, encourage and prepare them and their families for death.

John Wesley and the early Methodists spoke of having a "good death." In one of Adam's blog entries, he shares his thoughts on how to have a good, even happy, death. He would hope that his best sermon would be the one he preaches, not with words, but by his actions in his final days…and that people will say, "It really was true, he not only believed it, he lived it, and he was counting on it."

As we prepared to wind down our interview, we had a few last questions for Adam. Who is the first person you want to see when you get to Heaven and why? He was quick to reply that of course the first person he'd like to meet is Jesus. Among other things, he'd want to get answers to the questions he's always had. And he'd want to be rejoined with his grandparents, his youth pastor, and certainly Lavon and/or his children if they had passed before him. Other than that, there's no one specific because so many have passed on whom he's loved here, especially members of his church… too countless to call out individually.

We asked if he envisions himself continuing his ministry in Heaven. As he had earlier proffered a belief that we'll continue to have work to do, we felt this was a fair question for someone with such a great mission on earth. Adam believes there will be work to do, good and meaningful work. Whatever one's gift here, there will be opportunities to do that in Heaven. So yes, Adam hopes he will have a chance to minister in his next life.

As he had mentioned earlier that Jesus was the first person he wanted to meet because he had questions but didn't go on to share what those would be, we were curious and asked for some specifics. Without having to give it much thought, he said he'd ask how close we got to understanding the Trinity. And "why did You intervene in healing some and not healing others who were suffering? Mostly, though, he admitted that he anticipates being speechless, overwhelmed and in awe. "Although I understand time in Heaven isn't as we know it here." Adam believes your brain is released from limitations and you'll understand what we don't understand here, so it's entirely possible that there will be no need for questions at all.

As we did with many of those we interviewed for this book, we wanted to somehow incorporate food into the book due to the original reference to dessert in the Keep Your Fork story. When asked what food he would look forward to enjoying without consequence in Heaven, Adam's immediate response was that there was no single food that came to mind. He believes the joy of food here on earth comes from the fact that we can't have an endless supply without consequence. For instance, he pointed out that he keeps dark chocolate M&M's on his desk. The first handful is great, the second not as much, the third doesn't taste good at all, and a fourth will make him sick. So having only a bit of it is where the joy comes from. As the wheels kept turning, however, he became more animated and admitted to loving carrot cake...and with butter cream frosting, not cream cheese. He got this huge grin on his face describing it, like a kid describing a favorite toy or activity. In fact, he decided he would have to have some for dessert that night. As far as culinary delights in Heaven, Adam would love having carrot cake with butter cream frosting.

When Adam officiated at the funeral of that 3-year-old child on the day of our interview, he comforted that child's family noting that God was holding their little one in his arms. He reminded that child's parents of something Frederick Buechner once said: Because of the resurrection the worst thing is never the last thing. They would most assuredly one day see their son again.

Adam is a great leader, an example his church family is happy to emulate, and he profoundly believes in the certainty of an eternal life in Heaven. What we believe changes how we face death. For Adam Hamilton that can be summed up in the Apostles Creed...and its last line. I believe in...the life everlasting. Amen.

KEEP YOUR FORK

Carrot Cake

Ingredients
2 cups all-purpose flour
2 teaspoons baking soda
1/2 teaspoon salt
2 teaspoons ground cinnamon
3 large eggs
2 cups sugar
3/4 cup vegetable oil
3/4 cup buttermilk
2 teaspoons vanilla extract
2 cups grated carrot
1 (8-ounce) can crushed pineapple, drained
1 (3 1/2-ounce) can flaked coconut
1 cup chopped pecans or walnuts

Directions
- Line 3 (9-inch) round cake pans with wax paper; lightly grease and flour wax paper. Set pans aside.
- Stir together first 4 ingredients.
- Beat eggs and next 4 ingredients at medium speed with an electric mixer until smooth. Add flour mixture, beating at low speed until blended. Fold in carrot and next 3 ingredients. Pour batter into prepared cake pans.
- Bake at 350° for 25 to 30 minutes or until a wooden pick inserted in center comes out clean. Drizzle Buttermilk Glaze evenly over layers; cool in pans on wire racks 15 minutes. Remove

from pans, and cool completely on wire racks. Spread Cream Cheese Frosting between layers and on top and sides of cake.

Cream Cheese Frosting
3/4 cup butter or margarine, softened
1 (8-ounce) package cream cheese, softened
1 (3-ounce) package cream cheese, softened
3 cups sifted powdered sugar
1 1/2 teaspoons vanilla extract

Directions
- Beat butter and cream cheese at medium speed with an electric mixer until creamy.
- Add powdered sugar and vanilla; beat until smooth.

Faith to Last a Lifetime

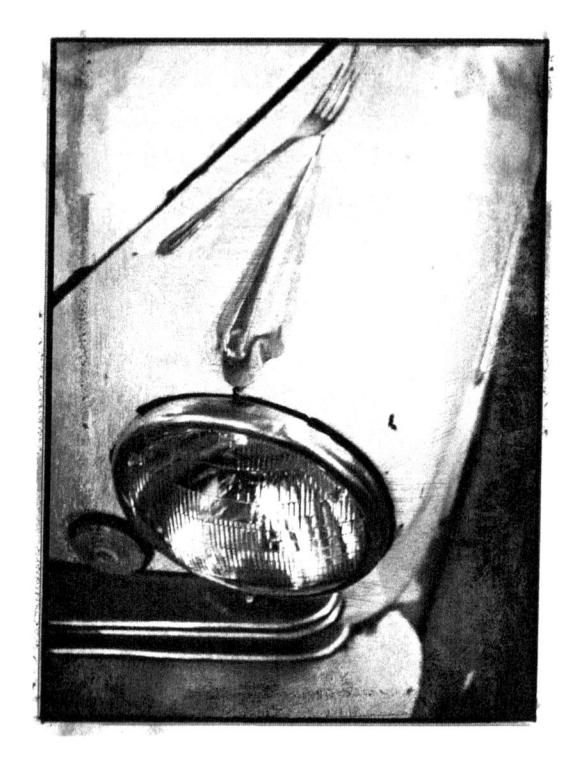

When I stand before God at the end of my life, I would hope that I would not have a single bit of talent left, and I could say, "I used everything You gave me."
—Erma Bombeck

FAITH TO LAST A LIFETIME

"My perspective might be very different from your granddaughter...or quite like her. The value in the story is how people feel the best is yet to come."

That is how Russ Creason started our interview.

I had the privilege of working with Russ for several years at a company where he didn't start working until he was 75. At the time of our interview, at nearly 94 years of age and with a very serious heart problem, Russ had just started to limit his work. He admitted that he didn't know how long he'd be working as his "mind works but [his] body does not." He seems physically fragile, his diminished stature one of the few giveaways of his advancing age. For if you merely sit and converse with Russ, his age is irrelevant. He's surprisingly clear and astute, and you can't help but get lost in his mind and his stories. And you can't help but be drawn to his ever-present, all-knowing smile. In spite of a formidable career that spanned seven decades, Russ' wisdom doesn't reside with his business expertise...though it is extensive. No, indeed his wisdom emanates from his heart.

Russ defies the stereotype of a member of the Greatest Generation. He is not bound by the ticking days on a calendar or the number of candles on a birthday cake. While his body betrays the secret of his eternal mental youth, his mind remains at its peak. He is a great storyteller, and there are so many to tell. From his modest (and at times even impoverished) upbringing in rural Missouri, through his college years that included a loss of credit hours due to after-curfew shenanigans, battling for our freedom in World War II, and an exhaustive business career that contributed to the huge success of one of America's premier success stories, General Motors.

Born at the end of World War I, he survived another World War, the deprivation of the Great Depression and the loss of many of his 12 siblings. He proudly speaks of having recently celebrated 68 years of marriage and a successful career that took him from teaching high school to leading General Motors operations in Europe and finally to human resources consulting.

The ebbs and flows of his father's career resulted in regular moves throughout his childhood. Even during times when his father was employed, there was never much money. His parents were Christians and raised their children with a love of God and knowing the power of prayer. The fact that they were able to raise 13 children through some of the most tumultuous times known to our country is a testament to living on faith.

FAITH TO LAST A LIFETIME

After graduating high school, Russ wanted to attend college, but his education was interrupted by World War II. Finally attaining his degree after the four-year interruption, he became a teacher...and though his career evolved to one of great prominence and success, he admits he's always been an educator at heart. Russ is a man of great humility. His roots are deep in family values and hard work. In order to get his degree, he worked odd jobs... mowing lawns, shoveling snow, clerking at a book store, maintaining a house for his room and board. He credits his success to his "just do it" philosophy.

Russ never imagined he'd attain success or wealth, yet he achieved both. He thought he'd be a school teacher, and in fact relished the dream. In reality, he was an educator no matter what shape it took on throughout his career. As an educator, a newspaper owner, a human resources professional and a business consultant, Russ' life has been spent on human development.

Faith became a very powerful force for him and took him through a lot of tough times. He recalls exercising faith when he was just 10 years old and his father was about to go bankrupt. He remembers clearly going out into the backyard by himself to pray for his dad. He didn't believe in praying by lowering his head and getting on his knees. Instead, he thought he should stand up and look up at God and talk to Him. And that's what he did...he asked God to help his father. The fact that his father did go bankrupt failed to diminish Russ' faith. His dad came out of it because he believed he would.

As he was coming to terms with faith and trying to make sense of it, he looked for the logic. How does a woman have a child like that? And then that child gets murdered and comes back to life three days later? His approach to life is rational, and he thought, "this ain't working." Yet while he couldn't reason the validity of these stories, people he respected believed in Jesus and believed in God; and that was a big influence on him. When he was about 20 and majoring in philosophy, he learned about various belief systems, as well as God's rules. Atheists believe in the big bang theory followed by evolution. He had no rationale for believing in Creation and Adam and Eve, but says his Christian friends believed that God created heaven and earth. Since in his mind somebody created everything, and the big bang theory doesn't make sense (who initiated the big bang?), he says it became fairly easy to believe in God.

This universe is infinite and human beings are finite. So that's a little system trying to describe a huge system, and we as humans can't do that. But it's there and knowledge is not only based in reason. Russ explains, "There are certain things I can know but I'm going to know them through this powerful thing called faith; so events happen and I just have to believe that it's God's doing and God knows what He's doing." Russ went off to war, and he was never frightened because he thought *I'm either going to come home or I'm not going to come home. But I believe I'm coming home.* He didn't have to wonder where that courage came from…it came from his faith. Certainly there were many more that had faith and didn't make it home. Russ knows he could have been one of them, but that reinforced this belief about faith. As an educator, he loves it that we continue to learn more and continue the exploration of faith and the part it plays in our lives. But he's not naïve enough to believe that we will ever know it all. It's God's work, and he believes God is changing the world and He has His reasons that we sometimes can't comprehend. And that is faith.

"Faith is the most powerful thing in life."

Those who know Russ would have no problem attesting to his legacy, but I wanted to see what he feels his contribution has been. He said, "My whole life has been devoted to developing people so that if I succeeded in that, that's a good contribution. In almost every venture 31 years with General Motors, what was I doing with GM? I was responsible for 200,000 people and I had to work not with them 1:1 but to build a system where other people would develop them and I would show them the techniques of how to do that and I would encourage them to do that and to make sure nobody was getting neglected." Russ' granddaughter, who has a degree in journalism, is teaching kindergarten….and the proud grandpa proclaims that she loves it. But he admits that as a high school teacher, he had looked down on the kindergarten teachers. He now realizes that the best thing we can do for our children (and for our future as a nation) is to focus on early development: Russ proffers that the biggest problem in our society today is not schools but parenting. Those first five years are critical, and we're sending kids with no development at home to kindergarten. They don't know how to behave; they don't know how to learn. *You have to nurture a love of learning from the very beginning.*

As our conversation turned to the afterlife, which I found difficult when speaking with someone who realistically is close to that eventuality, Russ allayed my discomfort with his typical rational approach to life: "Death is just a transition. You may or may not know that I have a terminal illness. At 94 why in the hell would I care? I've had a great deal. If you're truly a Christian why wouldn't you believe in that?" He doesn't understand why people think of death with such a negative connotation. The bad thing about death is that you lose somebody dear to you. That's reality. But the person we have lost is better off. Many of us have had loved ones who are so ill at 40 years of age that death is a blessing. Russ certainly wouldn't end his life, even if only for his own selfish good. "If I keep active, the two things I want to save about me until I'm no longer are my eyes and my brain. The body can go but if I can think and read and learn, that's great." Russ is a voracious reader and says he woke up in his 90's realizing he had neglected some very important areas about this world of ours. For instance, a recent realization as to the importance of physics (humans are chemical electronic systems) made him realize he had neglected to study that. So at 93, he's begun a study of physics.

In sharing his thoughts on the afterlife, Russ says he's unable to describe it. But that doesn't concern him because it's God's heaven, and for him to try to paint a picture of what it will be would be wrong. He knows for certain it will be a wonderful place, and we will have things to do. He believes energy is non-destructible so that when we die, the energy is simply moved into some other human being or to whatever God wants it to be. "Energy is indestructible. But that's on faith. The energy is our soul."

Following his transition, Russ believes we will continue to influence those remaining on earth but maybe in a different format. It would be a mistake to say it'll be like what it is here on earth. Maybe it will be, but not necessarily. And we don't have to know that. All we have to know is that it's there…that's faith…and that God's in charge. It's really a much more positive outlook. From this man of unshakeable faith, "We'll leave our bad behaviors and sins behind. That's what I believe."

I express my curiosity as to who he might want to speak with in Heaven. While he hopes this isn't true, he admits we might not be able to talk to anyone. But assuming he'll be able to talk to someone, he says, "Don't you think we ought to begin with Jesus?" And of course he wants to talk to Abe Lincoln (he actually said "of course", as if it were natural that this would be one of his first choices). But Abe believed in the things Russ believes in. And like Russ, he was a gentle man who was also very tough. He went through hell. He saved our country. With a grin on his face, he asked, "Wouldn't you love to talk to Einstein?" He thinks it would be great to renew acquaintances, but he readily admits he doesn't know that that's going to happen at all: "That's outside of our world. People do define what heaven looks like. Many religions do. I don't think we can do that and I don't think we have to do it. We just need to have the faith to know it's going to be a wonderful place. But when we get there we'll learn."

Three weeks after we sat down together, Russ Creason passed away. His body finally gave out though his mind was still as brilliant as ever. Russ was a product of his generation and the Depression, hard-working and honest. He was a gentlemen's gentleman. It gives me great peace to know that he approached his transition with acceptance, peace and even curiosity. As a lifelong educator and hungry to learn, it wouldn't surprise me if he was sitting with Einstein even as you read these words. For all of his numerous characteristics and glowing accolades from those whose lives he influenced, the most important facet of Russ was his faith. And he never doubted that while he lived a good and full and successful life…the best is yet to come.

Recipe for Love

Ingredients
2 Hearts Full of Love
2 Heaping Cups of Kindness
2 Armfuls of Gentleness
2 Cups of Friendship
2 Cups of Joy
2 Big Hearts Full of Forgiveness
1 Lifetime of Togetherness
2 Minds Full of Tenderness

Directions
- Stir daily with Happiness, Humor and Patience.
- Serve with Warmth and Compassion, Respect and Loyalty.

In the Moment

When the student is ready, the teacher appears.
—Buddha

IN THE MOMENT

Buddhism is one of those religions that for me is extremely misunderstood, or at the very least a bit of a mystery. Oh sure, there are the stereotypes: Buddhists look peaceful every second, they meditate for hours, believe in reincarnation, wear robes, are bald and sit in a lotus position. Many believe that Buddhism is not really a religion but a philosophy. Buddhism is certainly a religion, by any definition of that indefinable term, unless one defines religion as belief in a creator God.

Janet Nima Taylor is the Executive Director of the Temple Buddhist Center at Unity Temple. Having spent 25 years as a corporate executive in strategic planning, marketing, sales and training, she is now a licensed Unity teacher, former Buddhist nun and author. I can tell you that Janet meets none of my stereotypical expectations. Think Jane Lynch from Glee… you'd be very close to the woman who greeted us at Unity Temple. And after our time together, it's easy to believe that many…or none…of the stereotypes apply to a "typical" Buddhist.

Whereas many religions, Christianity certainly, are carried on from one generation to another, Buddhism is something one comes to as a means of self-actualization. Janet was raised Southern Methodist and as a young adult went through a period of atheism before having her interest piqued by Buddhism while in college. In her junior year she got to spend six months in India, where she became in interested in Buddhism and had her first week-long silent retreat. She admits to coming back to Buddhism after working in corporate America (she was broke and needed to earn a living) and two failed marriages. Getting ready to marry for a third time (to an avid KU fan), she needed to find someplace to get married on a weekend when the KU football team had an away game. She found Unity in the Yellow Pages. She's been there ever since.

> *"In 1996 a guy came in and said, "I want to start a Buddhist group," and I said, "Oh, I do, too. Let's do that." I remember working on the very first Buddhist promotional brochures. I was using my marketing skills for the good instead of the dark side. So Unity was really my ability to get deep into my passion. And in 1999 we had an organization called the Cornerstone Foundation. We brought in speakers and I met Wayne Dyer, Joan Borysenko, Deepak Chopra…everybody. It was so cool! And I was the person who announced them, so for five minutes I got to know all these great people. In 1998, I had been shopping around…I was ready for a teacher. I had tried out a few people who really didn't feel like a good fit. And here was Lama Surya Das (this big Jewish guy from Long Island who studied*

IN THE MOMENT

Buddhism for 30 years and incorporates his Judaism and Judeo-Christian stuff...he calls himself a spiritual slut), and, I don't know, he seemed kind of awesome. Okay, I'll go on a retreat with him. I went in January of 1999 and have been a student ever since. Now I'm one of his assistant teachers. So that's how it all just fell into place."

For Janet, Buddhism makes everything just "playful curiosity." About Buddhism she jokingly says she had a decade or maybe two of being a complete bitch, but Buddhism really has made her appreciate herself and other people, and turned her into a kinder and gentler person. So knowing that, the bottom line is that Buddhism keeps coming back to the present moment. What happens in the future is almost irrelevant, really. In a relative sense, what we are doing in this moment is what causes the outcomes in the future. We want there to be a better future, so we focus on being more available in the present moment. Being alive in this moment is really all there is.

Although raised Christian, Janet never really bought into the God-fearing philosophy of mainline Christianity. Growing up, she remembers if her mother really thought somebody was the best person they could possibly be, they were a 'God-fearing person.' But that just didn't innately make sense to Janet. Of course, as a child she had little recourse than to play along. She has distinct memories of doing so…and truly wanting to believe…because it gave her parents great comfort. They were dedicated and very kind, sweet people, but they definitely took the Bible literally and believed people were going to hell if they didn't take Jesus as their one and only savior. That certainly made life very easy. It's very black and white. If you do this, you go to heaven; if you do this, you go to hell. So there was a part of Janet that wanted to believe. For her 11th birthday, her mother had given her a little set of gold praying hands, one of Janet's most beloved material possessions. Praying before bed every night was a special ritual, and she prayed for Aunt Sally to get well…but Aunt Sally died. All the rationalizations began…it's God's will, God works in mysterious ways, etc. So when Janet sat down one night to say her prayers, she took off her necklace and placed it on the corner of the desk at the end of her bed, and she said, *"God, I'm not asking for much. I'm just telling you I'm struggling a little bit with my faith. I'm putting my necklace here. All I'm asking is that You just move the necklace from this side of my desk to the other side of my desk before I wake up. Then I promise I'm going to be a believer. I will have faith and I will buy in 100 percent. I promise, I promise, this is my commitment to you, God."* She got into bed, and pulled the covers up and she admits a part of her really hoped that the necklace would be moved because

IN THE MOMENT

then everything would be okay. But in the morning, the necklace remained where she had placed it. And that was the end of fundamentalist Christianity for her.

Unlike Christianity, Buddhism isn't about being a good person because of some fear of judgment by the bearded guy in the sky, but rather because of your essence. Janet believes everyone is innately wise, innately compassionate, innately loving. But life happens, and all of that goodness gets covered up with layers of trauma and abuse and violence and culture. At the end of the day, though, that goodness innately remains, even if dormant. Janet has grown to believe in what she calls diverse spirituality: we're all a religion of one. We all take from spirituality or religion whatever works for us. We may be saying the same thing, but we really all gather a spirituality that is a religion of one.

Janet shared a story about a young man in her congregation who was very dedicated to being Buddhist. His fundamentalist family was constantly trying to convert him back to Christianity because they believed he was going to go to hell because he's Buddhist, and that they risked spending eternity in hell if they don't try to convert him. Janet's teacher, Lama Surya Das, considers the possibility this young man's parents could be right. No one has all the answers. Janet appreciates that people have different perspectives and when she feels judgmental, she stays with that possibility that they might be right and she might be going to hell. it enables her to soften her perspective of them because otherwise she's as judgmental as they are.

> *"I just did a funeral for a congregant, a lesbian who had been with her partner for 29 years. They had met in a Bible study group and the other woman was straight; in fact was married with two children. The congregant had been praying for a relationship and for the right person to show up in her life, and she said that after about a year, this straight woman in the group said, "I think I'm supposed to be your partner." The congregant said, "Now wait a minute. We're not going to go down that road so easily because you're going to have to be really, really, really, really sure that you understand what that means, what you just said." A couple of months went by and she said, "No, I think I'm supposed to be your partner." And that was it. They fell in love and they were together 29 years. They were so loving and so caring, not only to each other, but they were chaplains, part of the prayer group, in the choir, helped everybody. They were both teachers. Everything about their life together exuded acceptance and love. You never know. You just never know…what if we could just all love whomever we love?"*

IN THE MOMENT

My co-author Misty shares that philosophy of acceptance and judgment, believing people have to live their faith. She doesn't have to live it or even like it. Misty explains her approach, *"Let me tell you how to teach someone how to love a lesbian couple that lives in their neighborhood: act just like everybody else. There you have it. There's the key. And, you know, I don't need to march in a parade or have my own special day or anything like that because I'm just like everybody else."* She has struggled with the polarity of being Christian and being gay. It's like she had to hit the "undo" icon on a regular basis in order to merge her Christian upbringing with her own heart and reality. She doesn't believe she's going to go to hell because she's a homosexual, instead believing that love is love. No one has the answer, so why make other people miserable because their beliefs don't fit inside your little square box. Because Janet discovered her independent belief system early on and dismissed the black-and-white Christianity of her parents, maybe she hasn't had to hit "undo" as often. She does admit to sometimes being a slow learner. That's why it took her until she was 48 to finally be able to be in a relationship. So whenever it happens, and with whomever it happens, it's good. You can truly be a Christian and believe in God and still be who you are, and it doesn't have to take anything away from your faith.

KEEP YOUR FORK

Janet candidly admits that she has trouble with the word God. As with many Christians, the word God was used as a bludgeon for her: God is watching over you, He'll punish you. The first talk she gave at Unity in front of 600 people, she spoke of how the word was hard for her to say. She professed this difficulty to her Buddhist teacher, and he took her to see his long-time friend Father Thomas Keating who at 90 has been a Trappist Monk for 70 years. He hangs out with the His Holiness the Dali Lama; did Zen meditation at a Benedictine Monastery in Massachusetts and got kicked out for it. Father Thomas told her, *"Well, you know this word God is just a placeholder. It's just a nickname."* And that loosened the lump in Janet's throat that developed every time she tried to say God.

Janet never used the B word (Buddhist) with her parents. At first they thought of Unity as kind of a cult, but after visiting several times, they decided it was okay. Her mom even sang in the choir. But they never said the B word. When her mom was 87, a year before she died, she said, "You know, Jan, I'm starting to wonder what this Buddhist stuff is all about; it seems kind of interesting." As Janet was her caretaker and had no one to leave her with, she had to take her to meditation with her. Janet described her little mother with a walker, the kind she can turn around and sit on, and they walked together to the Buddhist meditation room. At 87, struggling with dementia, she sat in that room for 30 minutes. When they finished, her mom said, "Well that was very relaxing. I ought to do that every day." Forty years later and she was finally able to say *yeah, this meditation is okay*.

In many ways, Buddhists are much like Christians. Some believe in reincarnation, some don't. When the Buddha passed into paranirvana 2,500 years ago, the idea was that life is suffering; some Buddhists believe that when we learn how not to suffer by acting in skillful ways, we are not reborn. As for her own perspective and experience in Buddhism, Janet tells us we are manifestations of this luminous, divine potentiality. We have this body, and this body hangs in there the best it can, but eventually the body wears out. The luminous potentiality, however, continues on. We each have an essence, the very core of who we are as beings. We get so attached to this body, to our sensations, our thoughts, and we identify as *'I am my personality, I am this body, I am these sensations, I am these judgments, labels, opinions, and all the other things that go along in our head and in our emotions.'* The Buddha was trying to disentangle us from this feeling of permanence because we're told that every seven years the body recreates itself. So who or what are we if every seven years we're something new? Buddhism doesn't lend itself to the idea that we have this earthly life and then we go someplace else. It is all a luminous void and we arise from it. Think of a flower as an analogy. Janet points to orchids in her office, and reminds us that they came out of the muck and the mire of the earth, and they grow into beautiful flowers. In a couple of weeks they will die (because she says she has a black thumb), and they go back to being mulch from which other flowers will be born.

There is a great joy in Buddhism for Janet in that there is a celebration of the preciousness of human life. We have an opportunity to cherish each moment because we don't ever know when it's going to stop. So, Buddhists cherish the moments of living, then death is just a part of the cycle of our essence, a cycle of living and dying where we never cease to be.

Death can be a blessing or devastation, depending on how it's approached or perceived. Janet shared two very different stories of how faith can affect the death experience.

> *"My mother's passing was the most fabulous death of anybody I've ever heard. She was 88, she had dementia, was really struggling in the last year. She had to go into a care facility because it provided 24-hour care, and she did the best she could for about eleven months. Then one night we got the frantic call from the memory care facility that she was having shortness of breath and that her heart rate was*

elevated. Though she had a DNR, the paperwork hadn't made it into the ambulance. Five minutes from the ER, she had a heart attack and they resuscitated her and intubated her. So, she arrived at the ER intubated and on life support. My daughter happened to be visiting here from India where she lives, which was just another blessing. The next day my family comes from all over the country, and we're all there and they were going to run some tests to see if her brain was functioning, what damage had happened to her heart, so we had a day of holding pattern. It turned out a great deal of damage had been done to her heart...80 percent of her heart was gone...there wasn't really any reason to worry about what was healthy in the brain. So my two sisters and I, the three of us, knew what Mom wanted to do. My mother had been so clear. While we all loved her greatly, it was easy for us to come together and say we would not want her to suffer. Then, we actually got to plan everybody to be there at 8:00 in the morning when the doctor was going to take her off of the breathing tube. We were able to all be around her and presumed that the moment the tube was taken out or shortly thereafter, she would pass away. We're all gathered around her bed and looking at her intently, and the doctor's taking the tube out and the Propofol's coming down and sort of in a suspended moment, my mother wakes up, looks around and says, "Am I in the hospital?" And we're like, "Yes, you are." And she says, "Oh," and started smiling. She looked around; everybody she loved was all around her. When she saw my daughter standing at the foot of the bed, she asked her, "Did you drive all the way from India?" My daughter laughed and said, "No, we just drove from Kansas City. I just happened to be here in the country." Here is a woman who had terrible dementia who was suddenly able to connect all the dots. My mom responded and replied, "Oh, okay, that's so wonderful. You know, this is great." And she started throwing kisses at people and joking around. She was just talking and lucid. We haven't seen her like this for years—having a clear conversation with us. She was getting a little tired when my great niece brought in my mom's newest great-great grandchild, Hazel, who was only two months old…my mother loved babies. When Hazel came in, she perked up and we propped Hazel up and took pictures of her, talking to the baby and exclaiming, "Oh, this is wonderful!" The baby was named after one of her sisters and it really was such a lovely, wonderful, positive experience. She was lucid, talking to

> *us, knowing everybody. She was having a delightful time. It's as if she knew this was a party for her. She grew weary and said, "Well, take Hazel. I'm kind of getting a little tired now." As she slept, we told her, "Okay, Mama, it's okay to go to heaven now. Your Geneboy (that's what she called my dad) is waiting for you. Your mother's there, your father's there. Half the family is already there." One day later, she died. How's that for an awesome death?"*

While Janet was able to share in a beautiful passing for someone she loved tremendously, she has a sadder tale to tell of a man she loved with as much fervor.

> *"I fell madly in love, as he did with me, with a man whom I was with for five years. We didn't want to get married, had already done that and both didn't do well with it. But we were madly in love so we just found each other later I felt like I finally got it right. He was diagnosed with cancer and he was given two weeks to live. He ended up living eleven months. This was in 2008 and I had just started working at Unity. He didn't have any need for spirituality, but he was the kindest, gentlest, sweetest person I've ever met in my life. He encouraged and supported me to take this job and to follow my spiritual path, even*

though it didn't mean anything for him. While I was doing church on Sunday, he'd go gas up the cars and wash them because that's what he felt called to do. But then when death becomes a reality at age 58, I would have hoped he would have had some reflection upon what was going to happen. One time during that eleven months he did ask me what I thought happened after we died, and I'd like to tell you I gave a very eloquent answer, but I really didn't. I gave him a short answer about what I thought and the possibilities. I told him he ought to go talk to Duke [Unity's Senior Minister]. He never went – he didn't want to talk to Duke about it, and he never came to believe there was anything after dying as far as I know. The last six weeks were miserable, particularly because he was fighting it with every bone in his body. He wanted to go home, so we turned the downstairs into a hospital room. We had hospice come in and I learned how to put feeding tubes in because he couldn't eat solid food. He was lucid and had every faculty about him, and the feeding tube was just feeding the cancer at this point. The pain was awful, and the feeding tube is very high sugar; so then he got diabetes, which meant we had to give him insulin shots. I'll never forget, I'd never done this, so I was supposed to prick his finger and take his blood and I couldn't get the little strip to get enough blood on it. I'm making this guy who's in excruciating pain even more miserable. He goes, 'JT, let's just pass on this because it doesn't matter.' Five days before he passed away, it got to the point where the hospice nurse said, "He's lucid. He can make this decision. But he has to decide to stop the feeding tube or this could go on for months." And so we all went down to talk to him about this difficult decision. He said he'd agree on one condition. He said to the hospice nurse, "Now, if I get better, you promise me you'll put that feeding tube back in?" And she said, "You have my 100 percent commitment." She took the feeding tube out, then we made him as comfortable as possible. But the last five days were horrific. He fought with every cell of his body because he truly believed that when you die, you're dead and you're done. For his family and friends, it was devastating to watch him in so much pain."

Buddhists don't refer to an afterlife as heaven because it isn't a destination; it's a continuation of the stream of consciousness. Underlying all this form, sensation, thought, and perception is a luminous intelligence or intelligent void, this potentiality. So we don't have to wait until we die to really be in that place. But maybe there is a place, a place where you go and have additional learning. Janet is excited about and open to that possibility. She firmly believes we're so much more than just this body. When she's telling her mother to go to see her husband, that makes both Buddhist and Christian sense to her. And she's okay with that.

The thought of an afterlife of sorts is very comforting for Janet. There's something more than just our bodies…there's our spirit. We're more than just our minds. Janet converted to Buddhism when she was in college, when she left behind the black-and-white approach of the Methodist Church she was raised in. For her, there was great freedom and peace in this ability to have this existence be all about spirit, about a powerful underlying all things potentiality. If we were freed from our bodies we would have a lot more freedom to do things that we probably can't do when we're encumbered by this physical form. But in Buddhism there's this idea that we don't have to wait until we die to experience a greater level of knowing. It's one of the practices Janet does in meditation, to actually have that experience of being inseparably interconnected and interdependent with all things so that nirvana ends up being this here and now sense of liberation. It can happen in this lifetime, even before you lose your body. In the West, we think of time as linear, and singular, but what if that is not a universal truth? What if there is the eternal NOW when multiple possibilities exist? What i there are multiple universes? Janet can recognize that there are so many possibilities that we haven't consider yet, and science cannot yet proved or disprove.

Janet's mother and her partner had very different deaths. It was their feelings about what was coming next that made the difference. Janet loved her partner whole-heartedly, and to see him suffering and fighting the inevitable…thinking there was nothing else to come…broke her heart. He would laugh at her saying this now, but she states, *"I feel his spirit is with me and I feel like he's watching over me. I feel like I can talk to him and that he figured out after it was all done, I think he knows now there is something more. I hope…"*

> *"I personally feel like people probably do have past lives. I certainly would love to get a chance to do a better job next time! Maybe life is like a school where you can learn a lot and keep making the world a better and better place. But, I know I don't have to really know for sure, to try and make the world a better place in this lifetime. The idea of reincarnation might come from my current limitations in "knowing". There might be millions of things that could happen after I die. I have a wonderful life. I don't want it to end any time*

> *soon. I'm having a heck of a good time living a "curious" life. That's enough for now."*

As the Buddha said, when the student is ready, the teacher appears. And that certainly was the case for Janet. She never would have thought in 1991 that she would have ended up at Unity doing what she's doing. But she can't imagine anything she'd rather do. "And if I die tomorrow, it'd be okay, but if I don't die tomorrow that'd be okay, too." She has had two lives: 25 years in the corporate world and now 25 years as a Buddhist and leading the Buddhist Center at Unity. Her life thus far has certainly been a "save your fork" experience because she never would have thought this is the path she would have taken. She says she would have been voted least likely to end up as a Buddhist minister, so you never know. Indeed, the best is yet to come.

Fostering Faith

Jesus said, "Suffer little children, and forbid them not to come unto Me, for of such is the Kingdom of Heaven."
—Matthew 19:14

FOSTERING FAITH

Blair Shanahan Lane was an old soul. An 11-and-a-half-year-old child who had a vision that few adults imagine, much less bring to fruition. Growing up with parents who took in foster children, Blair had ample opportunity to see the side of life she was blessed to never experience personally. Children leaving behind abusive homes or tragic events. Children who arrived at her home with nothing more than the clothes on their backs and a stuffed animal given to them by authorities as a means of comforting them during a confusing and stressful time. Blair wanted to know why a child would have a stuffed animal but had no socks on their feet. What started as part of her Girl Scout Gold Award project was on its way to becoming a nonprofit organization. While most girls complete their Gold Award projects as juniors or seniors in high school, Blair, not yet in sixth grade, was already filling journals with ideas and project plans for Foster Socks. That dream was snuffed out along with her young life on July 4, 2011…a life full of love, hope and generosity ended with a random bullet fired carelessly.

Blair Michaela Shanahan Lane was born two weeks late on January 24, 2000, after 31 hours of labor and two full hours of pushing. Her mom recalls reassuring herself with the reminder that God never said it was going to be easy, but He said it was going to be worth it. And Blair was definitely worth it. As her arrival in the world seemed to predict, she grew to be sassy, mouthy and wanting her own way. But she was also loving, generous and never held a grudge, giving people a second, third, and even a fourth chance.

Blair was raised in a family of faith. Michele Shanahan DeMoss raised her only child deeply steeped in the Bible and with a close relationship with God. For both of them, Michele says "there's just no doubt." Without hesitation, she describes her faith and her beliefs as a longing for Jesus Christ and the promise of everlasting life. When searching for a new church home, a 9-year-old Blair said, "Mom, this is it. I feel the Holy Spirit here." Michele wonders aloud why she didn't ask what that felt like.

Like her mom, Blair's beliefs went beyond attending church most Sundays, which she joyfully did. From a very young age, she lived her faith. Her generosity was great and showed a maturity beyond her years. She once gave a classmate her new bike because the girl didn't have one. A bike for a third child wasn't in the budget. But Blair had received a new bike for her birthday and she told her mom she could keep riding her old one. Blair had something she could give to make this little girl's life better, and she was more than happy to do it. In third grade Blair came home and bagged up a pair of her good tennis shoes to give to a classmate who had to sit out of PE because she did not have the right shoes. Blair said, "Mom, her parents can't buy her those." In her fourth-grade year she took all her birthday money and bought each student a book from the book fair. And she didn't understand why they had only two balls at the playground. She asked her mom why everyone couldn't have their own ball. That was Blair. Pragmatic. Compassionate. And determined to fix the problem.

July 4, 2011 began like any other 4th of July for Blair — she was celebrating the holiday in the backyard with family and friends just as she had since she was 2 years old. Blair suddenly collapsed. Had she been hit by errant fireworks? No...four nearby revelers had discharged a gun, and the bullet struck Blair. When she fell, Michele lunged forward and caught her. The blood stream so heavy, Michele sought to staunch the life flowing out of her precious daughter. Their eyes locked, and Blair mouthed, "I love you, Mom." And in that moment, there was no doubt whatever she was seeing that it was warm and it was welcoming. The look in her eyes guaranteed her mom *I will see you soon*.

In his attempt to comfort a grieving mother, Michele's pastor said that Jesus caught her. But Michele didn't need that reassurance; she already knew. Just as she knew that the same girl at the hospital who was fighting for her life knew she had a job to do. Even before she was legally pronounced dead, she knew she was

KEEP YOUR FORK

going Home. The only thing that still bothers Michele is the look of *why can't you come with me?* Michele knew that look because she had watched it when Blair drove away with people in a car; she wanted her mom to come along. She could see it in her eyes, and she could hear it in her voice. And to Michele, there's peace in not hearing that plaintiff cry when she said "I love you" as she lay dying in her mother's arms, the wound to her neck preventing her from giving sound to her words.

Blair was rushed to the hospital, and it was immediately apparent that she would not survive her injuries. She was placed on a ventilator so that loved ones might be present as she transitioned. When Michele finally got to her side at the hospital, she said, "Mama's here, mama's here." An unconscious Blair turned toward her mom's voice and started breathing on her own. She acknowledged that her mom was there! The bond between mother and child was that strong.

Hundreds of visitors came to the hospital, including friends, family, community leaders and pastors. Michele was amazed to see how many people Blair had touched. But her sweet child was not going to wake up, and all that was keeping her alive was a machine. Knowing her daughter's passion for giving to others, it was an easy decision to donate her organs.

FOSTERING FAITH

Shortly after Blair's death, a close friend shared with Michele a dream he had had. He described this very tall, beautiful, young woman wearing a white gown. Not a robe. A gown with lace – as if he was describing Michele's own wedding dress. When he saw her, she was sitting surrounded by children sharing their stories and then Blair got up and he pleaded with her not to leave. And she calmly replied, "Oh, I'll be right back." And she came back with a picture of Jesus and wanted him to share with Michele that she was safe. She stepped on her tiptoes, kissed his cheek, quietly did a little dance and said, "Next time you see my mom, give her that." But Michele is not worried. She is merely a mother who aches to have her child with her again. She knows without a doubt that Blair is not only safe but is rapturous in the arms of Jesus. It's that simple. But that conviction and the reassurance that's possible only through a strong faith do not diminish the pain she feels at the loss of the cherished child she loved more than anyone.

There have been times though where Michele has begged her to come home. She regrets that she wasn't clear about the address, because she knows Blair belongs to God and that she's gone Home already. She also knows she will join her before we know it; there's such a difference in understanding of time in heaven and here. What if only hours have passed for Blair? Michele has pictured her sitting at the feet of Christ and listening to the stories. She imagines the people she's with. She was always so inquisitive. She once wrote a paper in school about Satchel Paige. Did she go look for Satchel Paige when she got to Heaven? Her grandmother had passed away six weeks before B lair's death...did she greet Blair when she crossed over?

People say when one door closes, another opens. Michele believes it...even still. She likens it to crossing a pebbled creek. She's always been able to get from one stone to the other, gracefully. Even when it may have appeared to people around her that all hope was gone, she woke up and made the sun shine again. *I can see the sun shining. I can see the flowers are coming up.*

That optimism has been life-saving in the aftermath of July 4, 2011. Through the investigation, which ultimately led to the arrest of four men who were shooting off guns instead of fireworks; through the civil courts to extract some small justice for the premature loss of an innocent life; and now to state legislature...Michele's faith has remained a steadfast canvas on which God has painted grace and strength. Now Blair's grieving mother wants a change in Missouri law. She believes the crime that took her child's life should be a felony, and she hopes to call it Blair's Law.

FOSTERING FAITH

Blair is doing now in her afterlife what she always loved doing here on earth: giving. She never gave socks to homeless children, but as an organ donor, she may have given new life to at least 6 people, between the ages of six and 60. And, if Michele has anything to do with it, Foster Socks will not die with Blair. "Blair radiated the love and presence of God. She would have gotten this done," says Michele. "Now it's up to us."

As Blair's Foster Socks continues to grow and impact the lives of countless children in distressed situations, Michele works to spread the word about Blair's mission, her story, the power of organ donation, the goals of her nonprofit organization (www.blairsfostersocks.org), the dangers of negligent firearm discharge, and responsible gun ownership. The name of the organization belies a larger mission. Yes, some socks may end up with foster children. But Michele will readily tell you that we're all children of Christ. Blair, and now her mom, wants to support any child in distress situations. She and Blair would often drive by homeless people, and Michele would stop at a drive-through and return with food for them. At 4 or 5 years of age, that made an impression on Blair. She began asking for money because she wanted to give it to someone at the side of the road holding a sign. Yes, Blair's Foster Socks is much larger than socks. Through their efforts, children are learning that their current situation is not permanent, learning that they are a child of God, and learning to pay it forward. Because the Bible teaches us that we will be paid back tenfold.

Though not daily as in the months following Blair's death, Michele visits her grave often. She calls it Blair's Quiet Spot, and she finds great peace in spending time there…often heading there during a stressful day. What do you write on your child's headstone? Michele hopes another parent never needs to think about it, because she had three legal pages…*lover of life, daughter, sister, friend, granddaughter, stepsister, half-sister, cousin*… so many words that would be needed and yet insufficient to describe Blair. So she wrote only *Safe in the arms of Jesus*. And while she refers to this as Blair's final resting place, she also believes her real final resting place is with God in Heaven. She believes that although Blair donated her organs, which means her body was not whole when placed in her grave, God has made her whole again. There are also times of disbelief when she visits this sacred spot…hoping Blair will come down the hill toward her as if she's merely been playing a part in a film. Michele envisions somebody announcing, "And the Academy Award this year goes to Blair!" As she sits at her daughter's grave, Michele says, "Mom's here", and then remembers that of course Blair knows she's there. The wind blows when she speaks aloud there on the hill at Mount Moriah, as though Blair is screaming through.

Blair told her mom she'd make a change in the world. Not *I will change the world* but she would make a change. In only 11 years, she certainly did that and continues to do so. And she knew without a doubt that she would go to heaven. Blair has her final resting place, whether at the cemetery or in Heaven, and Michele believes she is in fact resting. But she believes, too, that there is an existence and a purpose for the people who've gone before us. And if we choose to believe that, then we know that there are no children in Heaven without socks.

Rice Krispie Treats
Ingredients
3 tablespoons butter
1 package (10 oz., about 40) marshmallows
OR
4 cups miniature marshmallows
6 cups Kellogg's® Rice Krispies® cereal

Directions
- In large saucepan melt butter over low heat. Add marshmallows and stir until completely melted. Remove from heat.
- Add Kellogg's® Rice Krispies® cereal. Stir until well coated.
- Using buttered spatula or wax paper evenly press mixture into 13 x 9 x 2-inch pan coated with cooking spray. Cool. Cut into 2-inch squares. Best if served the same day.

Return to Paradise

"Our life is love, and peace, and tenderness;
and bearing one with another, and forgiving one another,
and not laying accusations one against another;
but praying one for another,
and helping one another up with a tender hand."
—Isaac Pennington

RETURN TO PARADISE

Misty and I met with two Quakers, Gary Marx and Shane Rowse, in their place of worship. But there were no pews, no steeple, no stained glass, no vestibule or pulpit. We met on the front porch of an unassuming house nestled in an urban neighborhood after driving around for a bit trying to find a structure that would present itself as a spiritual meeting place. They had just finished their service and were putting away the folding chairs that moments earlier had been set out in a circle and occupied by a widely diverse group of people. There was no singing, no leader, no repetitive prayers said by the "congregation". Instead there was an open forum for sharing by anyone who felt compelled to speak. This is the Quaker way.

By way of introducing what Quakerism isn't, Gary opened our discussion by sharing a story about his 94-year-old father-in-law. An avowed "character" with some rough edges, he's known in some circles as Wild Bill. Bill lives in a small town of maybe 2,000 people, and every morning he meets his buddies at the local coffee house. Gary and his wife were visiting one weekend and accompanied him to coffee with his cronies. This preacher walks in, one of those very gregarious sorts of guys, talking and glad-handing and he comes up to Bill and says, "Now, Bill, we're almost ready for that steeple." And so Gary and his wife looked at each other as if to say 'what's he talking about?' You see, Bill doesn't go to this preacher's church. He doesn't go to church at all. He's in no way religious. And Bill says, "Well, they're building this new church south of town and it's kind of one of those pole buildings. And it looks a pole building." And that's what Bill told the preacher, that it looks like a pole building until you get that steeple on. And the preacher said, "Well I can't afford to put a steeple on our new church." And Bill said, "Well, I can afford a steeple." So that's what the deal is. He's going to buy a steeple for a church he doesn't go to. Gary and his wife were stunned and not a little confused. But when they found out what was behind his generosity, it made more sense. A couple of years ago Bill had a heart condition where he went to the hospital and he lost consciousness in the hospital and had to be revived. He came to and was really concerned because when he was under, he did not see the light. So now, you see, he's trying to buy his way into heaven.

The Quakers, or the Religious Society of Friends, began in the 1650s when a non-conformist movement was started by those who sought to distance themselves from Puritanism. The earliest dissenters went about seeking others of like mind and practice and were thus called "Seekers." When they met together, it was not to formally pray or preach, but simply to wait together for God to speak to them. Fast forward to today where we now find a number of different flavors of Quakers; Gary and Shane are Conservative

Quakers. Conservative Quakers are remarkably liberal politically, while the Evangelical Friends are the radicals, Quaker-wise.

Quakerism will vex you a little bit if you try to draw a circle around it, because one of the seemingly counter-intuitive things about Quakerism is that there tends to be a great distrust of dogma among Conservative Quakers. There isn't a Quaker creed, no Quaker gospel. There isn't a Quaker set of rules about what they believe. The idea is that there is a measure of the life God in everyone; that it can never be extinguished, although it can certainly be obscured. Consider Catholicism on the one hand, a huge monolithic edifice of dogma and ritual, and on the other hand is Quakerism as an empty room where they're trying to get rid of the dogma and the edifice. But the one thing that they've got in common is that in the middle you have mainline Protestantism that says God gave us the scripture and then split. There's this Bible and Communion. Quakers don't take communion. Catholics take communion and they believe that the host is actually, materially, God. Quakers take literally the idea of *"For where two or three are gathered in my name, there am I among them. [Matthew 18:20]"* It's not a ritual they do in remembrance of God; it's that there is actually a mystical event that happens. So on a lot of levels, Quakerism is a conscious attempt to leave open the possibility for that mystical experience and to get everything else out of the way. Shane shared a simple (he called it "silly") analogy that explains this concept a bit. *"I have a leather propeller beanie that I made, finest propeller beanie ever. And a lot of people ask why I don't put a motor on it. The reason that I don't is that if you put a motor on it, all you do it prove that it can't lift itself. But if you leave the motor off, you leave open the possibility that there's something you don't know about."*

While Quakers are trying to avoid dogma, they believe that if you are sincerely open to the Divine Will, you will be guided by a Wisdom that is more compelling than your own more superficial thoughts and feelings. This can mean that you will find yourself led in directions or receiving understandings that you may not have chosen just from personal preference. Following such guidance is not always easy. This is why community is important to Quakers: that community is their check and balance against running off the rails. The practical way they try to manage that is their belief that everybody has the light of God in them, and they try to seek that out in themselves and nurture and seek it out in others. As mentioned earlier, Quakers have no creed, gospel or rules, but they find that attending to the Light Within influences the ways they act in their personal lives, as well as the changes they work for in the wider world. They have discerned that certain values seem to arise more or less consistently when they try to stay close to the guidance of the Inward Teacher, and they call these principles their "testimonies." They are not so much rules to be obeyed as the outcomes of their efforts to live in harmony with the Holy Spirit. Some commonly recognized testimonies include peace, integrity, equality, simplicity, community, and care for the earth.

Quakers have evolved from the idea of talking about birthright Quakers because it is a thing that even if they were raised in it, they choose. A lot of people come to Quakerism after having bounced around a lot of religions. Shane was raised in a Methodist/Lutheran mixed family that was pretty "churchy." And when he looks at what he was taught from those traditions, he says Protestant Christianity comes down to original sin. That's the reason that Jesus matters and that is the means by which we gain salvation… which in turn lets us go into an afterlife that is a reward rather than a punishment. It all comes down to the fact that there is a stain on us from original sin that can't be removed but can be mitigated, at least periodically, by the regular application of sacrament…in the case of Catholicism, through communion, or in Protestantism, a ritual that is performed in the context of a set of rules that have been given the seal of approval by the Methodist conference. And then you've got Quakerism, which says you have a spark of the light of God in you that cannot be put out. And that is heretical because basically it is the opposite of original sin. So Quakerism, when you carry it out to its logical conclusion, started as a Protestant faith, but may not be Christian anymore. It may be when you follow that idea of the light of God within you, it may, in fact, go back to that period during Christ's life and immediately after Christ's death, where they were trying to find their way back to being that church. And that church wasn't concerned with the ordination of Christ; they were concerned with a relationship with God, that it's something that is present in all of us. And so Quakers tend to seek that inner Christ.

As a recovering Catholic, Gary was attracted to Quakerism by the community he found and the commonality of the people from one group of Quakers to the other.

> *"There's kind of an old hippy vibe in some aspects that I really related to. It's a very peaceful, open, listening community. I think I relate more to Quakers on a practice level than any sort of faith because when you get down to it, I probably have more akin to atheism than to Christianity. I feel at home here and I don't feel ostracized because I doubt the existence of a supreme conscious being who has this capability of relating to me as an individual. I think the concept of the light within all beings*

is something that I cannot explain. I recognize the existence of it. We can call it God, I'm comfortable with that. And we can call it something else, too, an energy force, a life force...whatever it is, I cannot define it. I don't think I'm capable or anybody is capable of defining it, but I recognize its existence and the fact that we are all connected somehow, even to animals. I've found a way here where I can experience that life form, worship it, or just enjoy it. And that's why I am here. For the practice that they allow this thing to happen, they accept me, and I think we're all on the same path. Maybe we're stopped along that path in different places. Perhaps it's an agnosticism, rather than atheism."

Human beings have this insatiable need to explain things because it is a chaotic world, and when you think about how small we are, it's a very frightening thing to some people to realize that life is going to last for 70, 80 years for some of us, if we're lucky. And to think that that's all there is frightens people. So the possibility of heaven or an afterlife provides comfort. But Shane feels that much of this concept of heaven and hell was a concept that arose as a way to keep people in line...a kind of quid pro quo spiritually speaking. If you do the right thing here, you get payback in the afterlife.

KEEP YOUR FORK

Quakerism has been described as a practical mysticism and also as being sort of Christianity's parallel version of Zen Buddhism or something. But Quakerism is one of the few faiths that Shane has run across where having an explanation of cosmology is not a foundation of the theology. The idea that God did this and God did that and God acts this way and we know these things about God isn't part of their beliefs. Quakerism is a little bit more comfortable with not having answers. And because of that, Quakers in general are comfortable with not having the church give you answers, telling you this is what God is. Answers are not the goal. The great reward as the carrot and the great punishment as the stick are not necessary either. And so they're freer to think in terms of the afterlife as an abstraction or, maybe it's there, maybe it's not. But it's not the reason that they're living and it's not the reason they behave the way they behave. So what keeps us all functioning as a society? Quakers say that God in each of us is enough. We are all members of the hive, and we are all working for each other.

Gary posed a thought-provoking question: if somebody gave you irrefutable proof today of the non-existence of God, the non-existence of an afterlife, would your response be to start robbing banks and kicking puppies and abusing your children? And if the answer is yes, then you don't deserve to get into heaven. And if the answer is no, then you don't have anything to worry about. The question of whether there's an afterlife is moot because if it's there, then who you are is going to determine whether you get in; and if it's not, and it changed your actions and made you a bad person, then it wouldn't be there for you anyway. The existence of an afterlife doesn't define who you are.

When Quakers talk about the things that they do, the good that they do, and the reward for those actions, it's not something that they displace into the future. Instead it is displaced into a sense of extended community. It's not so much the reward in heaven; it's having been part of building or being part of a larger or broader community. Even if the things that they do don't pay off for individually, they're part of something bigger.

Christianity with a capital c believes you go to heaven where nothing hurts and where no one hurts you and where you don't struggle. Gary and Shane think that in terms of their everyday lives it functions in the same way. There's a vision of being part of a bigger thing, of seeking out the light in others. *"It's a thing that you visualize and hold in your mind as a compass point, as a point on the horizon to aim for. While I'm sure that many of those people believe in that as a material thing, it functions is as a direction."* Maybe the reason that when you're angry you don't swat your kid is because of heaven, but if you look at what that does

KEEP YOUR FORK

for you, it doesn't matter what name you put on it… it's the thing that makes you better. And if you have to picture that as streets of gold and Elysian Fields or if you have to picture that as the world that you're creating here around you, it doesn't matter which. The end result is trying to be the best person you can be.

It is a common philosophy among Quakers that hell is not something God sentences us to; hell is a state of mind. You can imagine that to die and to suddenly be without all your money and cars and possessions, things that you're very attached to, would be hell because that's what you've identified with. You are literally in a hell of sorts not having those things anymore. So we've invented this thing called the afterlife where we can retain that life to which we've become accustomed. We're actually so attached to the material, ego and consciousness that we cannot conceive of letting go of that. So we have invented heaven, just as we've invented some of the old and now almost funny concepts of God, to make it easier on ourselves. If there's an afterlife, what is it that you take with you? For instance, if you have a nice guitar, the purpose of that is not having a nice guitar. It is being able to use it as an instrument of making music. It's not having this admiration of a beautiful thing and craftsmanship; it is the creative process that went into it and the beautiful music it creates. You'd like to believe that if somehow your consciousness goes on or the essence of you continues in some form in an afterlife. The thing that you take is not the guitar. It's the creative process of having used it. Each individual person is the center of their universe. Each individual person is the beginning; the life of that individual is the beginning and end of a universe. And if that's all there is, then you get to choose whether you make this heaven or you make this hell. And if something of you carries on, then what you chose to make of this is what will be carried on. And if there isn't, then you better make the best of it while it lasts.

Most Quakers challenge the notion of hell because of a shared belief in God as a loving deity not a vengeful one. According to Quaker belief, God's love is infinite, and the idea that he would punish individuals throughout eternity contradicts his nature. The Quaker God is a merciful one, and no sin is great enough to challenge this mercy.

Many Quakers would agree that the afterlife is more that that grand, greater place we go when we die. That inner light that we all have within is our essence. And when our individual existence ends, we cease to be an individual who's 'hi, I'm Jane, I'm a Quaker', but the essence of it goes on.

It was challenging to get Gary and Shane to talk about the afterlife, even though that was the reason for our visit. Because while they're passionate about life and about their beliefs, when they talk passionately about something, it's not about the afterlife. It was as if the afterlife was the sub-topic. The real topic is the nature of life and God. Human beings, the species, are members of the animal kingdom from a very scientific foundation point and looking at it from that angle. The thing that distinguishes us from most members of the animal kingdom is our ego…and that is a sense of self. That separates us from the rest of nature and it opens the avenue so that we can imagine killing other human beings. We can use the brain and we can use our hands so that we can do great harm to benefit the self and the ego. And that's where most of the ills that are created by humans can be traced to: the ego and how we use it. This gets back to their thinking about the Garden of Eden and how we started to imagine ourselves as being separate from God, being separate from Paradise, and we took ourselves away from there. We created great ill and maybe the metaphor of original sin can be traced to that sense of ego, that sense of self. We gave all that power to ego.

Perhaps after that separation, no matter how much we want our own ego, we're still trying to get back to Paradise, and maybe we've just turned it into heaven. We've turned it into the afterlife because we've separated ourselves; and maybe we still long for that sense of it and so we put faith, God, whatever you want to put into it, and we're still seeking it because we've been cut off from it.

Gary admitted that if he talked to his grandmother about the afterlife, she would have said you die and you go to a place. But today the discussion doesn't assume you go to a place. It goes to questions of cosmology and questions of metaphysics and questions of how we frame, how we make sense out of our existence in the first place. It's not about whether the streets are lined with gold or just really good brick. It is a question of the nature of our existence to begin with. What is the nature of the divine? What are we part of? Most Quakers have walked away from the idea that God's a guy or that God's a person or that God is even an entity. Instead they carry the idea of the inner light as a better metaphor of some greater thing that we're a part of and that we are a conduit for and are an expression of.

Humans have evolved philosophically, scientifically and spiritually. For example, in explaining the mystery of why the sun comes up, we invented this theory that one of the gods had a chariot and rode across the sky every 24 hours or whatever clock or time pieces they had at that time, if they had any. But we have moved away from those beliefs because our thinking and our theology have evolved. Those answers do not satisfy the questions anymore. The idea of heaven, hell and the afterlife is also a construct that we have invented. And perhaps those answers aren't any good either.

Gary's grandmother would have said we go to a place when we die. But we've evolved. The question becomes harder because the more information we have, the more we want to solve the mystery. And so we can't just solve it by saying we go to a place that might have gold bricks, that might be a cemetery, but we still can't solve it no matter how much we want to sit around and talk about it. Nobody's got enough information to solve it. That doesn't mean we're not going to try to solve it. It used to be a chariot that went across the sky and that's what took care of the sun. Now we have scientific knowledge that has told us what it is, and maybe we'll find something different than that later on as we continue to evolve.

Quakerism is a religion of life. They don't think a lot about death. Their focus is on the here and now. The idea of the afterlife isn't really about a place you go or thing you become. It's more a question of our inability to define God, but we can draw a circle around what God is and aim in that direction. Quakers know there's something bigger than them; they don't know what it is but sense that it's good. It's something that when they try to seek it out, it causes things to go smoothly and the world to be a better place and their life to work out…even when things aren't right. And

Gary says, *"Maybe that's all I need to know."* That's where their peace comes from. it's not having to feel that you need to do something in order to please the guy in the sky because it's innate, it's how you are and it's how you need to be and how you should be.

Misty and I got back in our car after visiting with Gary and Shane for a couple of hours, and our heads hurt from the shear depth of the conversation. We talked around and about heaven; we talked about science and philosophy and religion. People don't come to a Quaker meeting because their heads hurt, nor do they leave a meeting with a headache. It's a place where your head doesn't have to hurt. You can think about anything and believe anything… and it's okay. No rules, no dogma, no creed…no official leader to put a spin on a certain verse of The Bible. Quakers are people who are trying to return to that original relationship with God found in the Garden of Eden. Like Adam and Eve, they have an inner light of God that moves them to be the people God would have them to be. And hopefully that inner light will guide them back to Paradise.

KEEP YOUR FORK

Apple Pie

Ingredients
Double-Crust Pastry
1/3 to 1/2 cup sugar
1/4 cup flour
1/2 teaspoon ground cinnamon
1/2 teaspoon ground nutmeg
1/8 teaspoon salt
8 cups thinly sliced peeled tart apples (8 medium)
2 tablespoons butter or margarine

Preparation
- Heat oven to 425°F.
- Prepare Double-Crust Pastry.
- Mix sugar, flour, cinnamon, nutmeg and salt in large bowl.
- Stir in apples.
- Turn into pastry-lined pie plate. Dot with butter.
- Trim overhanging edge of pastry 1/2 inch from rim of plate.
- Roll other round of pastry.
- Fold into fourths and cut slits so steam can escape.
- Unfold top pastry over filling; trim overhanging edge 1 inch from rim of plate.
- Fold and roll top edge under lower edge, pressing on rim to seal; flute as desired.
- Cover edge with 3-inch strip of aluminum foil to prevent excessive browning. Remove foil during last 15 minutes of baking.
- Bake 40 to 50 minutes or until crust is brown and juice begins to bubble through slits in crust.

Miracle of Faith

A person's a person, no matter how small.
—Dr. Seuss

MIRACLE OF FAITH

Andrea Moskow is a beautiful, vibrant young woman, warm and welcoming, with a positive, upbeat attitude about life. Her smile can light up a room, and she is a spitfire. A good marriage, a career she loves and a gorgeous blonde, blue-eyed little guy named Jacob, she seems to have it all. But getting to this point hasn't been without its challenges and pain. A few years after losing her best friend in a tragic motorcycle accident, which she thought would be the worst thing to happen in her life, she experienced every parent's worst nightmare: the possibility of losing her child. Her strong faith would soon be put to the greatest test of all.

Andrea grew up in a nondenominational church and had a very strong faith and connection to God. Through some of her college and young adult years, she began to be a little unsettled, struggling with her faith; but she didn't know why. She admits that to some extent it was laziness...not making the effort to connect with God. Andrea doesn't believe you only go to heaven if you believe in Jesus, saying, "I don't feel that's how God would design it. He doesn't want that. I cannot understand Him not wanting everyone to be there. We're all children of God and God wants all the little children" to be with Him in eternity. Having gone through a yearning and an exploration of what God means, she attended a Catholic Mass and felt an overwhelming peace from God that this is where she needed to be. Little did she know the person singing and playing the piano was her future sister-in-law. Andrea married her husband in that Catholic church and even became Catholic in that church. It just felt like a good place, a good home. Andrea likes the formality of a Mass because when she is in times of crisis, it helps her to know where to start to focus. Her family struggled with her conversion, wondering if she now believed they wouldn't be with her in heaven. But for Andrea, sharing her husband's faith provided a means for raising their children in a similar background and faith. She doesn't believe that only one group or organized religion will be allowed to enter Heaven.

Andrea had started working with kids with special needs when she was 14, volunteering at the Lee Ann Britain Infant Development Center. Sadly, it was not unusual for them to lose children who had special needs. There was a little girl Andrea worked with who passed away when she was 7 but had lived longer than they ever expected. Also as a teenager, she nannied for a family who had a premature baby. Griffin was born at 29 weeks weighing 3.14 pounds. He stayed in the NICU for a lengthy period of time and came home on oxygen. There are lots of kids she's worked with recently too…"it's just incredible to see the strength and resilience in the families and the way they connect and the way they survive because they don't survive without each other. It's incredibly powerful."

MIRACLE OF FAITH

Andrea and her husband Adam were thrilled to learn they were pregnant in the fall of 2011. Her first trimester passed uneventfully, but she started having random preterm labor/contractions at 20 weeks. In order to allow the baby as much time as possible in utero, she was placed on bed rest. On Valentine's Day, at just 24 weeks pregnant, she went into labor. The baby was doing well, and vitals for both Andrea and the baby were good. But suddenly, he turned himself breech. And in spite of all attempts to stop her labor, her water broke, and his feet were already starting to deliver. She could see him, and he was bluish-purple and not making any noises. Jacob Thomas Moskow weighed 1.5 pounds. Andrea remembers there being so many people in the delivery room. The neonatologist started CPR counts for 21 minutes. It felt like an hour. She could finally hear...so many other things were going on in the room...but she could finally hear that little kitten sound, a little squeaking sound. They intubated the baby right away so the machine could breathe for him. At that point she knew he had breathed and they could keep him breathing on a machine. At such a premature birth, they hadn't expected him to breathe on his own, knew he would be on life support immediately. Once he was stable enough to go to the NICU, they whisked him down the hall.

Immediately when they had Andrea push, she started talking to God..."Don't let me lose my baby."

KEEP YOUR FORK

It's uncanny how certain things in life stick with you. Back in college Andrea took a child development class and they talked about the edge of viability for babies. Advanced technology could now provide pseudo-amniotic fluid for babies and that 24 weeks was the earliest they've ever had babies survive…at that time. She was fascinated with the technology and fascinated with the whole birth experience. Having lost little kids she worked with in the past, the tidbit of knowledge remained with her…and in hindsight prepared her for Jacob.

She knew when she was pushing that the chances of her baby surviving were not good, that Jacob might die. But they stabilized him and moved him to the NICU at Children's Mercy Hospital. The neonatologist came in with a sheet of paper, and she knew this was the formal conversation they had to have. She listened to all the statistics she already knew and didn't want to hear. The survival rate for a 23-week birth was 25%, and there was a 90% chance that he would have severe developmental disabilities if he survived. As soon as she could get them to release her (12 hours post-delivery), she headed to be at Jacob's side. She says, "There was nothing that could have kept me away." As she entered his room, she was directed to an isolette that appeared to be empty. She had to get right on top of it before she was able to see that there was in fact a baby in there…he was so tiny. This isolette was

MIRACLE OF FAITH

probably 2½--3 feet long and a couple feet wide and Jacob was 13 inches long. Every inch was covered with cords and monitors, and his little head lay on a gel pillow that kept his head shape. He was like a little newborn bird: translucent…"bizarre and scary."

Andrea fully admits that she wasn't the typical elated new mom. Oh, she was happy that she was a mom… but she felt she had let her baby down. As she sat by his side day after day, week after week, bawling and apologizing to him, one of his nurses approached her. The nurse was also a NICU mom when she was younger, and she said, 'I am really compelled to tell you that it's okay. I don't know why, but I feel like God put it on my heart to come up to you right now and give you permission to forgive yourself and to know that it's not your fault.' It was a pivotal moment in Andrea's process of being a mom to a preemie.

She constantly felt like there was an influence from God that was telling her things were going to be okay. For those first 24 hours she was expecting to lose her baby, but by the time he was stabilized in the NICU she knew he'd make it. Though terrified, and in spite of some scary days, once she saw Jacob in the NICU there was not a point in time where she thought they would lose him.

The morning after his birth, Andrea and Adam went to

see him, and his eyes were open. At 24 weeks that's unheard of. They had met other families that had babies born at the same gestation, and the babies' eyes were fused; their ears weren't fully formed. For Jacob to be completely awake, moving his eyes…this had to be God. So from that day forward, Andrea knew things would be okay. She expected to have challenges…there was even a point in time where she was planning to have a child with special needs in a wheelchair. But the fear they might lose him started to dissipate very quickly because his eyes were open.

Andrea and Adam are not only people of faith; they are surrounded by friends and family who share that faith. There were prayers from around the world…friends and relatives in different countries. Masses were said for Jacob in Rome…and the new parents felt the incredible power of prayer. I was amazed when Andrea told me that she and Adam felt so much closer to God during that whole process. We read about people who question God and their faith during times of trouble, and clearly that wasn't the case for these two believers. There's a Catholic church across the street from the hospital, and Andrea and Adam went every week for Mass. It provided a feeling of comfort during some unimaginable days.

Andrea was at Jacob's bedside all day every day, waiting and monitoring. Although doctors discovered a hole in Jacob's heart, surgery successfully closed it. At the time it was the second scariest thing, sending her 2-pound baby to surgery. But she constantly felt "he's here and fighting and every day he proved to us he was a fighter." She admits these were some of the hardest things they've had to deal with, but she felt an unexplainable peace because of the support of friends and family, even strangers...and God.

The family she had nannied for as a teenager played an especially important part of Andrea's life as the mom of a preemie. Molly brought Griffin to the hospital when Andrea was on bed rest, and he sat with her and watched cartoons and talked about the baby before they knew that Jacob would be born. Going through the preemie experience, Molly was her first source of reassurance and comfort as far as frustrations and fears. She came to the hospital and saw Jacob multiple times and was an amazing part of Andrea's survival and recovery. Having a baby in the NICU is so indescribably frightening, but Andrea felt comfortable very early on in changing him and doing things for him. She unequivocally credits that comfort to the time she spent as a nanny for Griffin...a child born at 29 weeks.

Jacob's birth immediately brought Andrea and Adam to God. She readily admits she wouldn't have had the strength to be there for Jacob emotionally, mentally and physically if she didn't have the faith and a strong connection to God. They felt the love of God through the people who were supporting them here on earth. It was absolutely necessary for them to feel that and to have that connection in order to get through what they were dealing with.

The ritual of Mass is the same no matter where you go, no matter what language. That's Andrea and Adam's foundation. And then they can go into the community from there and share Jacob's story…it's touched so many lives. Andrea hopes it always will because she has struggled with witnessing for others and trying to help show them how to live their faith. Andrea says, "It's an incredible blessing for our family to see the miracle he is. And now having seen this miracle I recognize the everyday miracles." It's made her so much more aware of the good things. Because you get in a slump sometimes…Andrea and Adam still do. But in the broad perspective of things, it has helped keep them in check a little bit…a reminder to slow down. And it's been a tremendous struggle and blessing for their marriage for she and Adam to be on the journey together…"The boat rocks and you figure out how to do it together."

While Andrea and Adam knew Jacob would survive, there was no way of telling what his quality of life would be until much later. He came home on oxygen,

MIRACLE OF FAITH

but he came home before his due date...also very impressive for a baby born so early. Jacob spent 98 days in the NICU, 16 weeks early and came home May 27...10 days before he was due. The fact that he came home before his due date is really incredible because the doctors kept telling them he had to be able to eat on his own before he could be released. Not only was he eating on his own, he was breastfeeding on his own.

You need not look far to understand what a miracle Jacob Moskow is. While he was in the NICU, Andrea and Adam knew three families who lost babies. Moms in the NICU bond quickly and strongly...no one else can know this experience like another NICU mom. They would share stories and concerns and strengths and accomplishments. Andrea shared the story of one family that knew they were going to lose their baby. They were from out of town a ways so had no close family for support. They wanted their son to be buried in a tux, and her family wasn't supportive; they didn't feel it was appropriate to bury a baby in a tux. So Andrea went out to Burlington Coat Factory and miraculously found a little newborn tux. She says that was one of the hardest things she's ever had to do, but if that mom wanted her baby to be buried in a tux and wouldn't know where to go to get it, Andrea figured "I'm just doing it." What can you do for somebody who's going to lose a child? After the baby died,

KEEP YOUR FORK

Andrea presented the gift as if it came from Jacob, and she was so thankful. You don't know what to do in such a situation, but in that moment it was very clear to Andrea that she could do *something*.

There was another little boy of Jacob's gestation who did not have the same development when he was born, and he lived only 9 days. There was another little boy of the same gestation, but he was significantly older when Andrea began her journey in the NICU. He was a year old when Jacob was there and was still in the NICU on a trach, and his condition would never allow him to be removed from the ventilator. This child remained in the NICU for another year after Jacob went home and passed away at 2 years of age. Some children born at Jacob's gestation had severe cerebral palsy, would never speak, would never walk, in some cases were unable to even roll over. They will be in wheelchairs as they get bigger. It's very apparent to the Moskows how different their experience has been compared to what's typical for that kind of gestation.

When talking to a person of such great and foundational faith, there's a natural segue to a discussion of heaven. Andrea believes Heaven is here, it's all around us because it wouldn't be haven for the people who are gone if they're not near those they love. Andrea says, "I wouldn't want it to be where I'm not near people…being able to see my loved ones." Although separated from them in a physical sense, heaven is still good.

Andrea and Adam became pregnant again in late 2015, and tragically their second child Jordan was born into heaven in January 2016. She knows she'll see this baby again and will then have her suspicions confirmed that Jordan was a girl. She had always felt confident about heaven being for real and knowing that she'd see people again. But it had been a fleeting thought…"oh yeah, someday." But now she has lost both grandparents, her parents are aging, having almost lost Jacob, knowing that Jordan is gone…there's still that emotional connection to them that she still feels their presence. Heaven is why she can feel that… whether it's in our minds or not, there's a reason why it happens. It doesn't matter what the mechanism is… if it's a mental connection, it's still real. People say 'oh it's in your head, you're making it up'. But Andrea says that's a whole piece of how it connects in itself. That's how we communicate with God…mentally, emotionally…not physically. And since God is in heaven, she suggests, "How could you not believe that something else is going on when you have that intensity of feeling and emotion and connection? I can't comprehend there not being something there. And when I'm there someday, I'll be the creepy stalker who's checking in and making sure everybody is good. I can't imagine it not being that way."

KEEP YOUR FORK

As she considers my question as to what heaven is like, she says she doesn't feel like it's a place because when you die your spirit lives on. There's not a defined geographical space because it's an existence but not a physical existence. So she feel like it's here, it's there…anywhere you can be, heaven is there. Yet it's beyond what we can describe or imagine because it's limitless. It's everywhere. Because she has her faith, she doesn't have to believe it's a place…it's not able to be defined because there are so many different definitions and variations of beliefs. No matter what religion you're talking about, the basis is love and existence and fellowship. She admits to wanting to know all the answers, but says she's "kind of okay not knowing."

When it's Andrea's time to be in heaven, she looks forward to seeing her loved ones again—but she enthusiastically admits she's anxious to see Jesus because she has so many questions. He's so forefront in Jacob's survival and she wants to praise and thank Him…"Thank you God for saving my son." She wants to talk to Him about peace and healing and understanding and comfort and love and joy. She says she can't even fathom how wonderful and amazing it would be.

But upon further reflection, she wonders how heaven can be perfect if she's there and her loved ones remain here. That's why she feels heaven isn't a place but rather surrounds us here on earth. What's important is the spiritual connection, the love, the presence you feel and when she's gone she imagines she would still feel that connection to her loved ones who are still in a physical existence. Having that connection still would bring her peace...being able to know that they can still feel her presence because she still feels the presence of those who are gone. Andrea believes "the body is the vehicle for this life, this world. But life is transcendent...life is before and after your physical body." There has to be peace in heaven...when we get there everything is healed. It doesn't make sense to her that when you get to heaven there's not some sort of connection and love.

"Truly, the experience of my son's birth and first years were so close to Heaven, especially in those first few hours and having felt the Grace of God in my son's strength and survival—I have never been closer to God/Heaven and the overwhelming joy and love that grew as my son showed progress. I can only imagine the joy to come in Heaven, once we are all there together...in His time of course!"

A lot of life experiences prepared Andrea to be Jacob's mom. The strength of character was shaped by what she experienced in losing friends, caring for preemies and children with special needs, comforting parents who lost a child…having had all these challenging things happen in her life. When she was young, all her friends were out partying and drinking; they hadn't had to deal with anything of these things. At the time, she questioned "why me?" In hindsight, she knows it was God's plan to prepare her to be strong enough for Jacob. He shaped her to deal with almost losing her child and not knowing what the future would hold.

When Jacob was born, Andrea never in her most positive moments thought he'd be the way he is today. When people who don't know his history meet Jacob for the first time, they look at her like she's crazy when she tells them he was born at 24 weeks and spent 3 months in the NICU. To this day, his physical therapist (and they've seen her for more than 3 years) always comments about how perfect his head is; that he doesn't have the preemie look. He was a chunky baby after he got off oxygen. He's starting to rough and tumble like a typical preschooler. The one noticeable effect of his premature birth is his ability to walk. He'll walk on his own but he'll fall a lot and get wobbly. But to his credit (and to the credit of his amazing parents), it doesn't faze him. He gets back up as quick as his mom can turn around, and walks off again. He's talking, smiling, becoming independent…very much a typical 4-year-old. And because he's your usual toddler, Andrea has to alter the way she parents. Up to this point, she admits to being very lax and cuddly (who can blame her)…

now she has to say no, you cannot play with the knives in the drawer because they will hurt you. No, you can't hit me and tantrum and throw things. But unlike most moms, she says, "It's so cool!" Yes, they have some challenges so she can relate to the families with special needs that she's working with. She can also relate to her cousins with their "normal" development of a 4-year-old. She talked to his therapist and described his behavior…and the therapist tells her "that's just a typical 4-year-old." It's music to her ears.

It's been a gray area on where Jacob is on the continuum of development. His mom doesn't know whether to give him a break because it's a sensory issue or whether to give him tough love…teach him to buck up and figure out how to do things. Jacob is slowly getting used to mom being one way before and different now. Even at bed time Andrea follows the same routine as Adam, but Jacob doesn't like it because that's not the way mom used to do it. But even with recent challenges and changes, Andrea readily admits that it's wonderful to see him coming into his own with his own personality…and she's figuring out how to be a mom of an ordinary 4-year-old.

Jacob is walking on his own, has some minor delays and some struggles here and there with gross motor. But the fact that Jacob is the way he is right now and not severely disabled in a wheelchair was probably around a 10% chance at the time he was born. His mom grins and says, "He is a freaking miracle."

Jacob's parents have a photo album of their time in the NICU, and he looks at it all the time. It's one of his favorite books. Andrea doesn't think he really understands yet that this is his story and that they all lived through this, but he loves looking at it. He recognizes mommy and daddy and pictures of grandparents and "the baby." He flips through and lets them talk about it. There are pictures of him with staples after surgery and he says "owie".

In February 2012, Andrea Moskow wouldn't have imagined the life she has today. They've come so far and have further to travel in Jacob's journey. She has God with her always, and she knows that Jordan is with her now as well. Sometimes it's our faith in God and the belief in something better coming after this life that brings us great peace and comfort in times of trouble. That connection to God and those who have passed on, yet remain with us always, gives us the strength to get up each day and put one foot in front of the other. Andrea's faith can not only move mountains, it allows her to climb over them. She and Adam hope to have another child some day. And while she will most certainly be anxious at times during pregnancy, she knows God gave her two children and Heaven knows, He can do it again.

End of the Line

*The battle of life is, in most cases, fought uphill;
and to win it without a struggle were perhaps
to win it without honor. If there were no difficulties
there would be no success; if there were nothing to
struggle for, there would be nothing to be achieved.
—Samuel Smiles*

END OF THE LINE

Everything works out in the end – and if it hasn't worked out, it is not the end.... this is Rev. Duke Tufty's motto for life and his journey into ministry.

Duke Tufty grew up in a fundamentalist Christian church and in the third grade was given a "Book of Prayer" that dogmatically asserted the theology of that religion... .'O thou great God, who art just and holy, I, thy sinful, unclean creature, come before thee in deep humility, confessing my many sins and my total unworthiness.' Can you imagine how frightening and confusing that was for a 7-year-old child? He says he was left with a sense of unworthiness, shame and guilt over the death of Jesus to the point that Jesus became the enemy.

The church of his childhood taught traditional definitions of heaven and hell where Heaven is a gold brick road with harps and angels, fluffy clouds...the ultimate paradise. Hell represented punishment and eternal damnation...the ultimate cruelty and torture. As he grew older, Duke found that he couldn't buy into what he was being told. As a child, he was frightened by the concept of hell and worried he wouldn't get into heaven. The God presented to him was a vengeful, punishing, disappointed God, and it seemed that all of humanity fell way below worthiness. His family mandated that you had to go to church until you were confirmed and then you could decide whether to continue going or not. Duke chose the latter.

KEEP YOUR FORK

Turning away from the church led him to a spiritless, anti-religious path. He walked down a road of destitution. When Duke was 22, his father died, leaving his son to take over his car dealership in Sioux Falls, SD. Suddenly he had access to a lot of money and freedom. He eventually expanded and moved to Kansas City where he found a much different culture...a culture where you get all you can from a customer because you don't care if you ever see them again. The goal was to wrap them up in long payments; there was lots of cash for deposits that never got recorded. Everybody used drugs. You came to work at 9:00, and when a car was sold a bell would ring and everybody headed to the back room to snort cocaine. Of course, the salesmen got excited to go out and sell another car so they could get another line. In short order, Duke became an addict and continued until he overdosed in Florida in a sleazy motel, lying on the bathroom floor. He remembers feeling that if he closed his eyes he'd never wake up. He kept counting the black and white tiles on the floor in order to stay awake. All night. Praying to somebody, not sure who, but he told God...he reverted to what he knew...if He'd get him through this, "I'll do anything." At that time he had two young children and wanted to see them grow up. He wanted to live.

And because God answered his prayers, Duke cut cocaine from his life, sold the dealership because that was the culture that put the monkey on his back, and started taking classes at a local university. He ended up broke and divorced...baking cinnamon rolls to make ends meet...and through his recovery he found a 12-step group at Unity Temple. He rankled against the confines of a structured support group and got up to leave; but on the way out he picked up some brochures that talked about spirituality vs. religion. There wasn't any reference to guilt, there wasn't shame, no dogma, no creeds. Only a message that this is the day you have to live your life, what are you going to do with it? Make it as beneficial as possible for you and for the world. He remembers it feeling as if a curtain was pulled open, revealing a sense of purpose and meaning. For the first time in his life, Duke pictured a reality he could create that was worthwhile...a reality where he felt worthy.

That image of a new reality led Duke to a theological college.. Despite his inauspicious past and what would seem a convoluted path to the ministry, Duke believes God called him while he was there. Fellow students would talk about reincarnation, places to go to read past lives, all glorious. While that was an interesting concept, Duke struggled with a realm outside the physical, concrete, present life we lead now. So when he left seminary, he started sticking more to science...and what it can provide to support his spirituality.

KEEP YOUR FORK

God kept knocking in his head that he needed to become a Unity minister. He resisted, telling himself "I'm not the minister type, I'm a car dealer." But God was persistent and reminded him of his promise on the bathroom floor counting the black and white tiles: I'll do anything. However, his desire and the plan of Unity leadership weren't immediately joined. The first time through the interview process, he got a letter telling him he wasn't their type. He was devastated…after all, he thought by following God's directive, his path would be clear. He did what he knew: he got drunk for six weeks and quit school. Unlike past downfalls, he actually took this as an indication that he wasn't ready for the ministry if this is how he takes rejection. In retrospect, he realized he had no experience in Unity Church or units to be a licensed teacher. This was God's message that there would be stumbles and squashed dreams along the path but that the journey would be worth it.

Back on track and sober, Duke volunteered at Unity on the Plaza. He applied again the next year and again was rejected. At that time, he had to decide whether find deep satisfaction in volunteering, or continue his pursuit of the ministry. He believes thoughts create reality, and that each of us can change our thoughts to change our reality. He was ready to accept that the ministry might not be his future. More importantly, he came to realize that most of the negative feelings he experienced were the result of his reaction to what was taking place and that he had to rise above that way of thinking. It became apparent that, in order to avoid certain mistakes and reactions in the future, he had to bring his thoughts to higher levels of spiritual awareness. Perhaps it was in that moment when God realized Duke was ready for the next steps in His plan or perhaps it was Duke's acceptance of the uncertainty of faith...but it was at this time that a new minister in charge of interviews pulled some strings and though only 30 students would be accepted, Duke got in. Following completion of the ministerial program, he was charged with a small church in Prairie Village. They needed more space and the congregation on the Plaza had dwindled, so Duke suggested they merge. That was over 25 years ago...and the rest, as they say, is history.

Life can certainly be challenging at times; there is no doubt about that. However, even in the midst of the darkest of times, we have the power to choose the effect the situation has on us and determine how we are going to respond. We have a timeline...our lifetime...with a beginning and an end. You spend your entire lifetime interacting with the world around you. Some experiences are very positive and feel very good, some not so positive and you feel bad. As you move on your timeline, you pick up thoughts and beliefs that are told to you and take them on as your own belief system. By the time you're 7 or 8, you have defined the world around you based on that adapted belief system. As you move into any sort of event or activity, the first thing you perceive is what's going on, followed by your mind defining it based on your beliefs, and finally you determine how you feel about what is going on. That's your reality, and it's yours and yours alone. Your reality is totally different than mine, mine is different than anyone else's. The beauty is that you're not stuck with the realty that was created for you by other people; you can change that reality, change your thoughts, move from sadness, sorrow or despair and heal yourself from emotional wounds of the past.

Our goal for our lifetime is a spiritual path where we elevate the highs and bring the lows up so they're not so severe until you gradually move up to the recognition that life is a wonderful, pleasurable event. Nothing can upset you or disturb you because you're the one who defines it and how you feel about it. How you react is up to you. If you have the old tapes going from authoritative figures who told you you were horrible and worthless, you believe that and as you move into adult life you continue to believe and get hurt again. Wound is torn open. Healing takes place that allows us to when we're reacting in a way that is hurtful to us, you stop and say is this the person you want to be? Do you want to be this hurt person not getting rid of hurt but accepting it as a part of myself? For so many years you condemned it and tried to get rid of it. When you approached it and embraced it, it got smaller and smaller until it wasn't there anymore. Your inner child was healed for you.

Duke reflects on the theory of some that 14 billion years ago there was the big bang, then nothing, and then a universe filled with energy that evolved into what we have today. The energy there in the beginning is the energy that's in each of us. We have skin, bones, organs, cellular structure, molecular structure, subatomic realm, and then energy...the same energy in you and me that was in the big bang. That energy is infinite, it never goes away. It just keeps reproducing itself in different physical forms. When the body is laid down, the cells and molecules lie down with it, but that energy of consciousness continues to exist. Does it meld back into the universal consciousness of the world? Individual and separate? Or is that an illusion? Duke says, "The best thing I can think of after this dimension is to have the consciousness that is me, put the drop of water back in the ocean and I become one with everything. In becoming one with everything, I lose a sense of individuality. I exist, but Duke doesn't exist, the personality is gone. Perhaps that drop of water can move into another incarnation. Perhaps I've done that, may do it again. It's like coming home. Imagine: surrounded inside and out by that which I am, by that which is all. The energy exists not in one place or another, but continues with no beginning and end...it just is." Duke's blending of science and spirituality is certainly obvious as he paints this ethereal picture of the afterlife.

As you can see by all that's been shared thus far, it's not surprising that Duke's perspective on the afterlife is also unique. Your entire life is spent with a belief system that is infused with an energy that has no beginning or end, and that energy continues to exist after the body is laid down. The consciousness you have here, the degree of peace of mind, the sense of well-being is that same feeling that will go with you. If you've had a terrible existence in this physical realm, unresolved hurt goes with you. That opens up a case for reincarnation. If this wasn't a good life and you got hurt and feel bad about yourself, that goes with you when you pass; but you have another chance to come back to work on that stuff so your world can continue to elevate to higher levels of conscious awareness and you're able to incarnate and create a heavenly state on this earth.

Several years into his ministry, Duke realized he had been obsessing about heaven to the point of not paying attention to the here and now. That was a huge turning point in his journey. Heaven is how you feel right here right now; hell is how you feel right here right now. Heaven and hell after this lifetime are the thoughts, feelings, attitudes and perceptions that go with you. Through Unity he was taught that Jesus was an example to follow and not an exception beyond human potential. Over time, He uplifted Duke to a beautiful new awareness of beholding the Christ in all people. He'd like to think when you move into the next dimension you can understand when daddy hit me and told me I was stupid, that happened to him too. Understanding deepens. Every negative feeling I have toward somebody, it's the result of not understanding who they are, what they've been through. They came into the world like everyone else, and the world created the person who exists today unless they step out and transform themselves. Lack of understanding is the only thing that can cause someone to have harsh feelings about someone else. Even Charles Manson…something happened to him along the way. He wasn't born that way.

There's no need to spend a lot of time thinking of what the next life will be. Salvation is now—not something that occurs after death. Heaven and hell are states of consciousness, not geographical locations. We make our own heaven or hell here and now by our thoughts, words, and deeds. Jesus encouraged those who had suffered a great loss and were grieving the death of a loved one to realize there is no separation in Spirit. They would be reunited with their loved one in time,

KEEP YOUR FORK

but first they had a life to live here and now. And that life should be lived fully.

From the ups and downs in his family's car dealership business, to a drug overdose, a time not knowing the next step, and finally a slow but steady climb into ministry, Duke tenaciously created himself from the quote of Winston Churchill's "Never, Never, Never give up!" Jesus inspired those who were downtrodden with heavy burdens to stand tall and walk confidently. He assured them that they had all they needed to make it through difficult times. Duke's faith has shown him that three paths exist, and every person can choose one for their life paths.

One path is that of a conceited person, the path of arrogance. On this path you need to convince others that you are better than them to get their admiration and respect. You need to be right. You need to be the best.

A second path is a never-ending battle to get others to see you as "better," and you dislike those who don't. This path is a lonely embittered one because you don't believe that which you expect others to believe about you.

The third is that you are a human being no better or worse than any other person. This is a path of inspiration and admiration for those who are a beneficial presence to this earth and one of compassion and caring for those whose value and achievements aren't evidenced by riches, power or fame. This path of life feels like home, with all people being a part of your spiritual family. It is peaceful. It is pleasant.

The path Duke follows through life is one of humility, for that is what he was taught by his childhood religion. He learned that prayer of humility in Sunday school—"O thou great God, who art just and holy, I thy sinful, unclean creature come before Thee in deep humility confessing my many sins and my total unworthiness."—and he believed it to be true. As a result, he felt like a disappointment and failure who was less than others. His path of life is a sad and demoralizing one, void of purpose and joy.

Contrary to some religious beliefs, Duke believes we were not born sinners, and there is no need for us to be reconciled with God…because we are not separate from or in disfavor with God. Each of us is an expression of God Spirit…of the oneness that exists with each of us and God…"life is an experience of the oneness that exists with you and God." As Duke shared his path, his beliefs and his convictions, I was reminded that there is a difference between spirituality and religion. While he is a Christian minister, Duke is more aligned with spirituality than religion.

KEEP YOUR FORK

There are two basic ways to know what the true religion is. The first is to let another or others tell you. In most cases their response will be "my" religion is the only true religion. Support for their dogmatic assertion will come in the form of fear-based notions, which purport that you are a sinner, that you will never get to heaven and that the only way for you to be "saved" is by following the doctrines and creeds of their religion. The list of persuasions goes on and on. The more a person, religion or pronouncement holds to the arrogant position of proclaiming it is "the only true one," the greater the proof is that it isn't.

The second way for you to know what is the true religion is to personalize it and do research to discover what the true religion is for you. Determine what empowers you and resonates with your deepest beliefs. Your spiritual path should be one that impassions you, not imprisons you. It should be one that continually moves you to higher levels of joy, love, peace of mind and harmony. Seek and you will find the spiritual source that is best for you…the one that truly supports your greatest happiness and highest good. And the more I know about Unity and Duke Tufty, this second option is a depiction of their spiritual religion.

While Duke believes in and follows many of the lessons found in The Bible, he also believes there are many holy books like the Bhagavad Gita, Tao, Koran,

Torah and Dhammapada that provide similar direction and inspiration for life. Each holy book provides a uniquely different spiritual path, but all paths move in the same direction and have an identical destination.

Duke Tufty is an enigma. I sat down with him assuming I would hear from someone who could think outside the box. Unity is not a typical mainstream religion full of dogma, rules and stifling adherence to specific verses of The Bible. And I wasn't disappointed. Yet there are very mainstream Christian beliefs there as well, and he shares them freely. But instead of coming across as dogmatic, his message is one that runs parallel to the bottom line of The Bible…love one another. Jesus made it very clear that He was the example and not the exception. The peaceful, loving, and harmonious approach He took toward life can be taken by others as well. That includes you and me. All we have to do is choose it. As Duke says, everything works out in the end – and if it hasn't worked out, it is not the end.

Heaven on Earth

*No one is useless in this world
who lightens the burden of another.*
—Charles Dickens

As we planned this book, one of our goals was to include the perspectives from as many religions as possible. As a recovering Catholic, I certainly wanted to share the story of someone from that religion, and who better than a nun. But if I thought selecting Sister Berta Sailer as a stereotypical example of a Catholic nun would result in the story I had anticipated, I learned I was wrong almost as soon as we sat down together for the interview.

Sitting behind her paper-strewn desk in her basement office, surrounded by photos of smiling children, Sister Berta greeted me warmly but wondered aloud what I thought she might be able to contribute to a book about heaven. I thought it odd coming from a nun, as I recalled my childhood educated by nuns in habits who had no hesitation in sharing views on religion and heaven at every opportunity.

First impressions might lead you to believe Sister Berta to be more suited to education or perhaps spoiling grandchildren than running an operation that has grown to the size of Operation Breakthrough. She has that take-charge aura about her tempered by a calm voice and easy smile, and in her late 70's it's clear that she has had a life well-lived. But it wouldn't take more than a few clicks of a mouse to discover what it took to get here…and that Sister Berta is most certainly up to the challenges she faces every day.

KEEP YOUR FORK

Talking around no less than a half dozen interruptions…phone calls from home, staff needing a signature, an introduction to someone from the UMKC Bloch School of Business who's writing Operation Breakthrough into a grant …in fact the phone continued to ring even during that introduction. Sister Berta is a busy woman.

There's no way I can do service to Sister Berta's accomplishments, but I do want to at least lay some groundwork for how she landed where she is today. She was raised by her grandmother in Chicago after her parents died in a car accident and, seeing this example of selflessness, has spent her adult life seeming to make each step a deliberate effort to help those most in need. It's just who she is and what she's always done. But as for why she became a nun she says, "I have no clue. What makes you decide something at 18?"

In 1971, she and Sister Corita Bussanmas recognized needs in their community and co-founded Operation Breakthrough to provide childcare and other social services for working-poor families in Kansas City. In the beginning, the sisters had an informal arrangement to watch a handful of kids whose mothers could not afford child care. They named it Operation Breakthrough for two reasons: they were going to break through poverty, and, being that it was during

HEAVEN ON EARTH

the Vietnam War, they thought the government would think it was part of the war effort and would give them money. That didn't happen.

This not-for-profit agency is now the largest single-site childcare center in Missouri, caring for more than 600 children each weekday who come from homeless shelters, foster homes and struggling single parent families. As I made my way to her basement office, I had passed the daycare center full of laughing children and several bustling staff members smiling as they went about their busy days.

With too many programs to enumerate, Sister Berta spoke of their Starfish program that is facilitated in partnership with area churches. In explaining the name of the program, she shared a story about a man walking along the beach picking up a starfish and throwing it back in the ocean. Somebody pointed out to him that there are too many for him to save, and the man replied, "I made a difference for that one." The mission of Starfish is to get middle and upper class women to meet the Operation Breakthrough mothers, believing that once they spend time together, they will discover they're just alike. One of the Starfish mothers was a Certified Nursing Assistant who couldn't find a day job. She had two kids and she took several of these women with her to the food stamp office one day, just as a friend might do. There were four HR people who were members of the church who had positions available in nursing homes. The Operation Breakthrough mom had a job in two weeks. We all use networks; but if you're a poor person, you don't have a network. If a mom has so many issues, she can't see tomorrow. Getting these groups to meet each other is the answer.

That's why their mothers do so poorly: it's a situation of "us and them." When the spinach scare was in the news a number of years ago and we were told we'd die if we ate spinach, their food pantry got a thousand cans of spinach donations. What makes you look in your cabinet and say *it could kill my children but I'll give it to them?* Sister Berta firmly believes that if we could get rid of poverty in this city, we'd solve education, we'd solve crime, and we'd solve a lot of the drug problem.

Seeing how hard these mothers try and seeing them succeed in small steps is the most rewarding part of Sister Berta's life at Operation Breakthrough. Two moms recently got their GED's. Her staff says she has an "old lady conspiracy theory"…they've made the GED test harder so their mothers can't pass it. "If every kid in this building went to college, who would flip our hamburgers? Would we still have dollar burgers? Who would make our beds at hotels? A job is a job, but people should have opportunities. The kid who could cure cancer could be in this building and we better make sure his family can feed and house him and give him a place to sleep."

State legislators in Jefferson City are very familiar with Sister Berta; she attends legislative sessions regularly. In fact, she imagines a balloon above their heads saying, "Here comes that crazy nun from 31st Street." If we really cared about these kids, we could change this if we chose to. She once told a legislator she could fix the system for him. He looked at her like she had no brain and asked how. Her response? "Give every foster kid a puppy and get the animal rights people in here and we're done."

Sister Berta has seen more tragedy in these past 40 years than most of us could imagine. They've buried quite a few children...some as children, some as teenagers who got shot. But there are a lot of success cases as well. Three Operation Breakthrough kids whose mother is an addict have been adopted by an attorney.

She will talk endlessly and passionately about our economically-segregated society. One of her primary missions is to get upper and middle class people to meet these women, fully believing they would find out how similar we all are. Her office sees a constant stream of people in need. Their problems run the gamut from homelessness to domestic abuse. Admittedly some of the moms at Operation Breakthrough have

KEEP YOUR FORK

issues, and some might even be truly lazy and unmotivated. But she's pretty sure the same could be said for some millionaires. She operates within the rules that make sense–those of compassion and generosity.

Sister Berta and co-founder Sister Corita have gone beyond their work at Operation Breakthrough in supporting children in need. They are licensed foster parents and have adopted four children ranging in age from 11 to 18. Sister Berta knows what needs to be done and will stop at nothing to ensure it happens. She has made the children of Operation Breakthrough her life, personally and professionally. Pointing to the picture wall in her office, she says, "We have to make sure these kids have a tomorrow." The little boy in the red shirt, Chuck, was one of her foster children. He came to them as a 4-year-old after having watched his mom's boyfriend kill his little sister. One day as she drove past a fire station, Chuck, strapped in his car seat, said, "if I grow up, I want to be a fireman." He said *if I grow up* because he didn't assume he would. Tragically he was right. He went home when he was about 7 or 8 to live with his grandmother and later joined a gang. He would come back to visit Sister Berta periodically, and with her support, he decided to quit the gang. He was shot to death in his front yard for quitting. And when the man who killed his sister is released from prison, his mom plans to marry him.

HEAVEN ON EARTH

Stories like this are too numerous to share, but they all point to the bottom line: If there's no tomorrow, it doesn't matter what I do today. Who cares? Sister Berta believes we have to give families a tomorrow because it *does* matter what happens tomorrow. "We save tin cans and we throw away children. And that worries me."

Since 1971 more than 10,000 youngsters cared for while their moms work. You look at the picture wall in her office, and it's astonishing…photos of success stories mingle randomly with photos of those who were provided a foundation at Operation Breakthrough, only to be lured into gangs who provided acceptance and purpose not found anywhere else…shot dead in their own neighborhoods. They are all her children. When the sisters couldn't figure out how to help enough just by taking care of children during the day, they opened their home. Over the years, they have officially fostered 75 children. They adopted four. Living with the sisters today are eight young black kids ranging in age from one to 25, including a non-verbal teenager in a wheelchair, born addicted to 12 different drugs. Some of the kids have lived with the nuns their whole lives, some are foster kids and some just come and go.

With such dire situations to deal with day in and day out, one would imagine that faith plays a great part in maintaining optimism and moving forward. But since Operation Breakthrough gets Head Start money, they can't mention God or heaven or religion at all. About 15 years ago two guys flew in from Washington to see if there were any religious items in the building. While unable to talk about religion, Sister Berta tries to encourage their families to do what's right and to make good decisions. That's all religion basically is: treat your neighbor right. Their research for their Starfish program revealed that every religion in one way or another says you're supposed to take care of your neighbor. "So why aren't we?" she wonders.

Sister Berta grew up Catholic and in fact attended Catholic schools from elementary through college. She's unsure if we're rewarded for good deeds when we die and firmly believes the reward and punishment concept is used by religions to manipulate children. A lot of churches lead us to believe that we'll go to heaven if we sit in the pew. Sister Berta thinks you have to do more than that. "I think a lot of people say *'here's a can of green beans.'* That's a help but you have to make sure that when stuff comes out in the paper that will hurt families you have to stand up for it. Religion is more what's inside you than what you do." She believes the answer is in getting churches to do what they're supposed to do. And make a difference for their neighbor.

HEAVEN ON EARTH

Sister Berta is a nun, a leader, a parent and certainly a force to be reckoned with. She admits that she's not a good long-range planner, preferring instead to tell the truth in love and let the chips fall where they may. She's a woman of great humility. Whenever I would comment on the good she's done, she always deflected with "a lot of people help us."

Through all the worrying and all the tough times, she's always able to laugh. But she is well aware of her responsibilities. Asked how long she can continue working so hard for so many people, a flash of exhaustion crosses her face. When they adopted children, they didn't think about how they'd raise them on Social Security. She has to make sure the young kids finish school, and she'll work as long as she can to provide for them. She says, "so far I've been pretty lucky." I believe it has little to do with luck.

As our discussion turned inevitably to heaven, Sister Berta's first reaction is that whatever it looks like "that's gonna happen after we die, maybe there will be some equality. There isn't much here." She admits that she doesn't spend a lot of time thinking about heaven. If you sit in her office for five minutes, you'll see why she doesn't have a lot of time to ponder the afterlife. She once heard a preacher say our job is to make heaven here on earth. And that's the philosophy Sister Berta has adopted...because she knows we're a long way from it. Although she's a Catholic and a nun, she hasn't spent a lot of time figuring out what's there, although "I probably should because I'm getting old." She prefers the idea of making heaven here on earth… because this life can be hell, especially from her vantage point. If we made the city like heaven, there would be no socio-economic boundaries, no need for the messaging around poverty and no need for an Operation Breakthrough. Perhaps everyone in heaven would be like Sister Berta.

When pressured for something concrete on her image of what heaven will be, she pictures a place where everybody gets along, there's no economic disparity and people are at peace with each other. People can use the gifts they have because the picture of heaven as sitting around playing harps is stupid to her. She'd rather have her description of heaven actualized here on earth. She concedes that heaven might involve "going up in the clouds somewhere" and that when she dies she'll find out she wasn't right about her expectations. Whatever that next life is, she hopes to be with her grandmother who raised her. Now that she has reached an advanced age and is taking care of children, she recognizes how hard her grandmother worked to provide a home for her. Her grandmother worked at a laundry, ironing. Yet after working all day, she'd take Berta by bus to the beach. She was on her feet all day and she was probably the age Berta is now.

HEAVEN ON EARTH

Berta calls her a "tough cookie" and credits her with making her the woman she is today. So when she sees her grandmother again in heaven, she wants to thank her for all she did, and for sticking with her.

However she spends her time in heaven, I can imagine her doing things alone without people tugging at her. Though she has spent a lifetime doing for others, she's not comforted by a heaven where we relax and do nothing but rather have another opportunity to use our God-given gifts and talents. She's open to the probability that heaven will be different for each person, conceding that what's heavenly for her might not be heavenly for someone else. She'd like to have pets and horses. She hopes to go fishing without children, as her fishing days ended once she brought children into her home. Fishing with kids is just a series of putting worms on and taking fish off. She'd like to *really* fish. Perhaps there will even be an opportunity for reincarnation. If so, she'd like to be born to a family of a millionaire so she'd have money to do more than she's been able to do thus far. She hopes to get to heaven but knows if there is a hell "they're going to make me the head gardener because I hate to garden."

The sisters have been taking care of kids for 42 years. Today, Operation Breakthrough is serving its third generation of children. Thirty-five of its former kids are now in college. The once seat-of-the-pants daycare has a professional CEO and an $8 million budget. Inside its walls are health and dental clinics for children, a periodic health clinic for adults, a food pantry, mental health services, GED classes and a staff of social workers to support families.

Sister Berta, now in her late 70's, puts in 10-hour days, but admits she is also slowing down. From the start, the sisters wanted to give the kids in their home a normal life. And in some ways they've succeeded in keeping them out of the fray of the kind of tragedy they see at Operation Breakthrough. She's accepted that making heaven here on earth won't happen in her lifetime and even admits that she doesn't know if it can ever happen.

Sisters Berta and Carita will leave a legacy with dozens of kids who lived under their roof at one time or another. Their legacy also is permanent at Operation Breakthrough, though it is widely believed that once they are no longer there, the organization with never be the same.

Sister Berta Sailer is a surprise if you meet her with the expectation of expanding the stereotype of a pious, dogmatic, steeped in religion Catholic nun I was introduced to in my childhood. Sister Berta is strong, opinionated and passionate, not afraid to laugh… at herself or religion. She does what she does not because of a vow she took at 18 but because she believes it's the right thing to do. She believes we are all put here on earth to make a difference in the lives of others, and she gives selflessly of herself in order to walk the talk.

She may not believe heaven on earth is possible. But then, there's always a way. That's Sister Berta's motto.

Criss-Crossing Dimensions

And those who were seen dancing were thought to be insane by those who could not hear the music.
—Nietche

Take a moment to call to mind an image of a psychic. Flowing, colorful robes, wild red hair (for me, the hair is always red), looking into a crystal ball, laying out tarot cards, incense burning, extravagant jewelry, asking generic leading questions to draw responses that will provide enough information for her to make "predictions" so you'll believe she's for real. Or perhaps you think of the Long Island Medium with lacquered bleach-blond hair, fake nails and flamboyant personality. If that's what you're prepared to experience from a psychic, you would be surprised to meet Glennie Turner.

Glennie greets us at the front door of her aptly-named "hobbit hut" for our interview. Hugs all around, we are escorted into a beautifully-appointed living room that welcomes us like a hug wrapped in a well-worn quilt. Her precious dog Nicky made himself comfortable at my feet. Nowhere to be found are incense, tarot cards or crystal balls. And Glennie is certainly nothing like I described a stereotypical psychic. She is all at once your favorite aunt, your best friend of 40 years and a trusted advisor...a mother or a grandmother even. Immediately you feel as if you can trust her and share your innermost thoughts, fears and wishes. Which is good...because, as we discovered, those things will be revealed to her anyway by those who show up during our session.

KEEP YOUR FORK

Glennie has known of her gift for as long as she can remember. Since Glennie was a very small child, she has known how to sense and communicate with souls that have passed over. When she was a little girl, she thought everybody could see people walk through walls, that everyone saw beings of light. She thought it was natural until her girlfriends told her they didn't see what she saw. Her grandmother advised her: "Keep this to yourself, Glennie, as the world isn't ready for you yet." She can often find missing items and people, sense if one's surroundings are positive or negative, see and interpret beautiful colors around one's body, have dreams that come true, and has had out-of-body-experiences. She believes there is a much higher power in control, and she calls this higher power Divine Spirit."

> *"My first experience was when I lived with my great-grandma. A big old beautiful home, front porch with a swing on one side, and glider swing on the other for the boarders she took in and cared for. There were people coming and going all hours of the day...including some that were ghosts.*
>
> *Did I see ghosts all the time? No, but I do recall one day sitting on the front porch swing with my great-grandma. She was shelling peas for dinner that night, when I saw a man*

walk up the sidewalk, stop on the porch steps and look at us swinging. I will never forget the sweet smile on his face. I immediately said to my grandma, "Grandma, who is that man standing there?" She looked, then told me, "Glennie, I don't see him. Tell me what he looks like." I went on to describe him and when I looked up at her, a tear was coming down her cheek. She said, "Sweetheart, you just described your great-grandpa and I think he has come to let us both know he is doing just fine and watching over us." As she continued shelling her peas, she went on to tell me some stories about my grandpa.

I remember being very content with her answer and when I looked back to where he was standing, he smiled, and then he walked through the screen door into the house with all the other living and deceased boarders."

When you're meeting with Glennie, you're never alone with her. There is no on/off switch for her gift, and periodic visits are made by those who choose to come forward from the other side. Mid-sentence, you'll hear that slight intake of breath that signals the presence of a guest, and she'll ask "who is Jason or Jay" or "who is Nick or Mick with stomach problems, still here?" At first it's quite disconcerting as your mind

KEEP YOUR FORK

inventories loved ones to determine who wants your attention. But it quickly becomes at once exciting, comforting and often emotionally-charged.

As we attempted to move down our list of interview questions, it soon was apparent that this would be a discussion unlike any other. One interruption mid-thought occurred when "Margaret" and "Susan or Susie" came forward prompting Glennie to ask "who's writing the cookbook?" Well, Margaret is my mother, and Susan is my aunt. And part of the initial plan for this book was to include recipes as a nod to the original story referencing dessert as a synonym for the best yet to come. As we delved into our interviews and unearthed such rich stories, that part of the plan got sidetracked. But it was obviously not something we were meant to leave out of the book, and my mom and aunt wanted to remind us of that.

Glennie provides great comfort and healing to those with whom she has sessions. No stranger to tragic losses, it's not only Glennie's gift that gives her the empathy to comfort her clients. She lost her first love to the Vietnam War, her husband and a brother to suicide, and her best friend to a drunk driver. While so much tragedy might taint one's perspective, these events have merely given more depth to her beliefs about life, death and the afterlife. Her ability to connect with those who have passed over has afforded her the opportunity to keep her loved ones not only close to her heart but present in her day-to-day life. Glennie is a big believer in signs. Her beloved dog Nicky often confirms the presence of spirits in her home with a bark and a glance in the direction of the spirit.

Glennie is not only visited by the loved ones of her clients but also by her own. After her brother's death, she was very angry because he had committed suicide. Not long after he passed, she was sitting at her computer and it froze while she was doing some research. It stopped on Woodward (her maiden name) and then she saw the name he was called that shouldn't have been in the material on her screen...and realized her brother was there.

People come to Glennie to connect with loved ones and she acknowledges that it's very rare for a loved one not to come through...they *want* to come through. Sometimes they want to ask for forgiveness. Sometimes people will ask Glennie what their departed loved one wants to tell them. But what if mom or grandma isn't going to tell the truth or might misguide you? Glennie's spiritual discernment comes into play, and if she doesn't think this energy is good, she doesn't say out loud what she's sensing.

This intimate knowledge of the afterlife prompts one to wonder if her gift resulted in her strong faith...or if her faith allowed her to accept and share her gift with others. A self-proclaimed spiritualist, she believes God is love. Underneath that spiritualist umbrella she's called a psychic medium, admitting candidly, "If I see something, I'll tell you. But I don't like to go dark; why go evil?"

As any conversation with Glennie includes the afterlife, it's natural that we would also query her about religion. A belief in some sort of afterlife doesn't always mean heaven, and we were curious as to the role of religion in Glennie's journey. Her grandmothers were Christian, and her mother was raised in a Christian home. Glennie's father's family was Baptist, her mom's family was Methodist. They allowed Glennie to go to any church she wanted to go to, but her family never forced her to go to church. However, she admits she felt very connected in church: "The first time I went to Sunday school, I had chills all over. There's true divinity and spirit there. It's only the man-made stuff that got away from that." As Gandhi says, "'I like your Christ, I do not like your Christians. Your Christians are so unlike your Christ."

Faith has always been with Glennie. Of an afterlife, she has experienced paranormal or other worlds or out-of-body episodes. So she believes there is a different state of being, another dimension. What she does not believe in is time and space…everything happens

CRISS-CROSSING DIMENSIONS

at once. She shared a beautiful and comforting description of the afterlife:

"When we cross over, maybe we're crisscrossing another dimension. We are energy in pure form. It's a continuum of energy from this dense matter. Once you shed your body and go to that other dimension, there are several different paths, different places you can go to rest. I believe we go to a sacred garden where we do have a life review with all these beings of light around us. We have two spirit guides from the time we're born. If there's a hell we might have to see what we did that hurt someone deeply and how we made them feel."

The more Glennie studies, the more she realizes she started out in the Bible—"Jesus saw angels, and I did too!" Glennie believes in angels and beings of light. They help us to understand our mission on earth and they are forever. She believes people who have crossed over can be spirit gods. When she talks to people, she tells them the hardest thing to do is to not beat ourselves up for being human. She's cautious with whom she shares things…"If I'm at Wal-Mart and see negative energy, I don't go down that aisle." As we're told by John in the Old Testament, Glennie says she is in the world but not of the world.

KEEP YOUR FORK

When we cross over there is a light that resonates of love and a peace we'll never feel here. The rainbow colors around people's bodies are phenomenal. [*"Misty, you have a huge gold circle around you."*] Heaven could be different for each individual. During one of her out-of-body experiences, Glennie saw on the wall a huge vortex open up. She saw different sized beings with different size circle halos around their heads. The gatekeepers were the tall grays. The beings in those other realities are so different.

Many believe that someone who takes their own life have no place in heaven. Glennie reminds us that having a perfectly healthy body doesn't mean we have a perfectly healthy brain. No one would leave a family behind if they knew what really happened. "Sometimes I think it's merciful." We're encouraged to take care of our bodies, but as a society we're not comfortable with how to take care of our minds. Glennie's husband was brilliant in the corporate world yet hid his depression from the outside world…certainly the severity of it even from her.

Glennie doesn't believe someone who commits suicide goes to hell. Rather the minute they cross over their angel comes to comfort, not scold. Hell is us having to view in our human form how we made someone else feel. If we know we've made a mistake, suicide or not, mental health or not, and we don't do it again, that's what we're here to do...to learn and to not make the mistake again. She doesn't use being human as an excuse. Whether you're committing suicide or dying by another means, don't use it as an excuse...you're only human. Human minds are frail and can get lost. They don't go to hell...their hell was here.

Those of us who have lost a love one long to reconnect with them in the afterlife; that's the only way we have to be with them again. Though Glennie can and does connect with her loved ones who have passed on, she still wants to be with them once she crosses over. She'd give anything to bake oatmeal cookies for her daddy or shake her finger at her husband. She's only human and if you really love someone, that love never stops being.

Her father showed her how to die beautifully. She asked him to be with her after he died...wanted to actually feel him and smell him. She once heard knocking (and Nicky looked in the direction of the knocking, his ears forward), and her dad's voice said, "honey I'm busy, we went fishing enough and think of all the times we fished." As soon as the door shut, Nicky sat back down. Glennie says, "When I hear, I pay close attention."

When she thinks of the afterlife, Glennie sees herself

sitting in a boat fishing with her dad or sitting around listening to his stories or watching John Wayne movies. She'd like to see her boyfriend who died in Vietnam, just "meld into the energy of the love we shared." She would like to sit in the sun with her husband, go to the covered bridge again, and sit in the park of their youth.

What she doesn't believe about the afterlife is the existence of hell. She firmly believes that "here is hell." She's talked to people with near-death experiences, and they've experienced hell. Thoughts will create reality; and if their religion believes in purgatory or hell, that's what they'll experience. But Glennie's God is not a God who would condemn us to everlasting pain and suffering. Her God will take us to a garden and say 'come here honey, let's talk about this.' People on earth are putting us through hell now. If you had asked her when she was 30, she would have said there's a bearded man sitting in heaven and He's going to condemn to hell those who don't believe what she believed. When she was an evangelist knocking on doors, there came a point where she had to stop because she didn't believe in the message she was sharing. She awoke one day and said 'I can't do it; I don't believe in hell.'

Glennie also believes in reincarnation and that we have a choice as to whether or not we return. I mentioned earlier that on the other side there are different paths. One of them is to return in human form. She believes in multi-dimensions, that this isn't the only planet where life exists. We can go anytime we want to reincarnate here or any other parallel dimension. While the media depicts reincarnation light-heartedly by implying we can come back as a dog or a cat, Glennie pooh-poohs that. But she does believe a loved one can create that love in a creature. She's not sure why we come back to be human other than we want to learn more about humans. Those who continue to evolve consciously understand that they are spirit and exist to learn as much as they can and then return. As a voracious learner with a hearty curiosity, Glennie says she'll have to come back thousands of times.

Without prompting, Glennie asked Misty and me, "Do you know how many lifetimes you've known each other? You really were supposed to meet. You've been together lifetimes." It seems that Misty and I lived together in the old south prior to the Civil War in the early 1800s. Misty was black and I was white.... and my father owned her father but was not cruel to his slaves. Misty died on that plantation, and I mourned her death. We were both female and very close friends. I ended up being a teacher. That particular tidbit is ironic as my husband's family is full of teachers, and I've always felt like I was a bit of an outsider. Apparently we have more in common than we realize.

KEEP YOUR FORK

Glennie knows that she has had many past lives and has re-experienced many of them. She shared a fascinating story in which she was regressed two lifetimes. Having had chronic popping and cracking in her jaws and diagnosed with TMJ, she learned during the regression session that in one lifetime her husband broke her jaw. She saw a dear friend there who was unable to say anything because women couldn't speak. After that regression, her jaws never hurt again.

She had recurring dreams as a child of a young woman named Mary with a long face, thick waist, her hair up, wearing a long dress with a high collar and high-top boots. Glennie could feel herself putting on boots and saw her sisters and collie dogs. She went over to a mirror to fix her hair and what she saw made her gasp. It wasn't her own face but Mary's. For three days after the last time she dreamt it, she felt the high-top boots, the high collar. A short time later, her aunt made copies of family photos and Glennie saw a picture of her great-grandmother Mary...and it was the woman in her dream.

Glennie is not afraid of the afterlife. Her own personal experiences show her that it's beautiful. She's able to comfort her clients with reassurance that their loved one is not suffering and did not suffer in death, because she knows that the minute their soul passes on, there is no suffering.

CRISS-CROSSING DIMENSIONS

There is great evil that exists on earth. It's somehow comforting to imagine that Hitler made it to heaven and was returned to this planet to create something more harmonious. Glennie knows that if she were in God's shoes, she would dust him off and tell him, "you didn't get this right at all; you weren't put here to kill thousands of Jews." She wouldn't send someone back as a snake or a snail...I would send them back in a form to do something great and good.

Glennie admits to having her own demons that she has to fight every day. Every day she gets up and starts over. Her life appears easy living in her hobbit hut world, but she struggles like all of us. And in her own words, she is "more human than anyone in this room." She returned to her childhood home town of Sedalia, MO, and for a time it was her Shangri-La. But two people she loved and adored have left her side because the church says she's the devil. She's been grieving that loss for over a year. She misses her friends and family outside the area. She's hard on herself, expects a lot from herself...and I get the impression that her gift contributes to that need to do more. She gets mad at herself for getting mad, for being human. But Glennie has people and spirits and her little Nicky who love her. And there's nothing as important in her world as love.

Glennie recently undertook a project to close out the

KEEP YOUR FORK

old year and ring in the new. She began reviewing the journals she had kept over the years; and as she read her own words – words in black and white regarding the journey of returning to her truth and who she really was – she saw within those words a woman "unbecoming what she never was." The pages revealed the emergence of The Knower. Within each word she saw a woman making a major transformation in her life. She saw and felt within herself the dance of grief that she had to do to become the authentic Glennie. She was reading about the transformation from darkness into light, and the embodiment of the courage to step into her own heart's desire.

> *And those who were seen dancing were thought to be insane by those who could not hear the music.*

Many people have thought Glennie to be insane, and some still do. She has loved this Nietche quote for as long as she can remember. She definitely dances to a tune not too many people can comprehend. But she lives the life she has chosen to live… a life filled with people who, like her, are knowers…gentle souls who know what love is all about and what it is not all about. As Ernest Holmes says in The Science of the Mind, she has learned "the Light of Life is full within me and around me." And all is as it should be.

Worm Food

The fear of death follows from the fear of life. A man who lives fully is prepared to die at any time.
—George Bernard Shaw

WORM FOOD

Not everyone believes in God. For some, an afterlife is not a believable or viable concept in which to place trust. Wanting to cover as many perspectives as possible for *Keep Your Fork*, we didn't want to include stories of only mainstream, organized religions with a clearly evident belief in God and some sort of afterlife. So we found an individual who is prominent within the atheist community to share a perspective that is completely counter to the premise of this book: there is no life after death; when we die, we're "worm food."

What is atheism? The reason no one asks this question a lot is because most people have preconceived ideas and notions about what an Atheist is and is not. Where these preconceived ideas come from varies, but they tend to evolve from religious influences or other sources.

Atheism is usually defined incorrectly as a belief system. Atheism is not a disbelief in gods or a denial of gods; it is a lack of belief in gods. Atheism is not a belief system nor is it a religion. While there are some religions that are atheistic (certain sects of Buddhism, for example), that does not mean that atheism is a religion. Two commonly used retorts to the nonsense that atheism is a religion are: 1) If atheism is a religion, then bald is a hair color, and 2) If atheism is a religion, then health is a disease. A new one introduced in 2012 by Bill Maher is, "If atheism is a religion, then abstinence is a sexual position."

KEEP YOUR FORK

Darrel Ray is a leader in the Atheist community, a published author, and the Chairman of Recovering from Religion. Recognizing that many people are reconsidering the role of religion in their life, and many more feel negatively impacted by religion and faith, Darrel saw a need for a place where they could go for support in finding a new direction. He describes Recovering from Religion (RR) as a safe landing place where you can believe what you want. Many people come to a point that they no longer accept the supernatural explanations for the world around them, or they realize just how much conflict religious belief creates. It can be difficult to leave religion because family and culture put so much pressure on us to stay and pretend to believe the unbelievable. The mission of Recovering from Religion is to help people find their way out. As Mark Twain famously said, *"Faith is believing what you know ain't so."*

Darrel was raised a fundamentalist Christian in Wichita, Kansas, by parents who eventually became missionaries, and among family members highly involved in church life. He attended church with his parents three to five times a week, his father was an elder, and his grandfather was a country preacher for 45 years and one of the founders of Westside Church in Wichita. Darrel was baptized at 9 years old as an Independent Christian, a subset of the fundamentalist Church of Christ. They believe a person goes to heaven only if "dunked." His grandmother was convinced she was the ultimate authority on scripture and theology. He learned very early never to argue with granny for fear of being slapped. Another great example of loving Christianity that stayed with him.

Darrel has a vivid memory at age 12 going New Mexico to visit relatives who were reservation teachers but actually saw themselves as government paid missionaries to the Navajo Indians. They climbed a mesa and found shark teeth scattered about. Fascinated, he began putting them in his pocket and showed them to his mom and aunt, curious as to how they got on top of the mesa. He was told God put them there in the flood. Darrel knew even at that age that this was nonsense, and that moment began his journey to skepticism. Though surrounded as a child with bible-believing Christians, he never bought the creation story or the story of Noah and the flood. He admits to being a pretty skeptical kid, but he kept going to church on Sunday because he loved to sing in the choir as a soloist. He even started learning how to preach a bit and in fact preached from the pulpit of his own church while still in high school.

Following graduation from college with a degree in Sociology and Anthropology, he went on to get a master's degree in church and community and ultimately a doctorate in psychology. Throughout his education,

KEEP YOUR FORK

Darrel's interest in religion began to fade. He would have stopped attending church altogether, but he had married and started a family...and his wife believed fervently that their children must go to church. He found the most liberal church they could both tolerate, which outraged their parents. Though he was an agnostic by this time, he wanted to keep peace in the family and still loved to teach and educate. So he became a Sunday school teacher, teaching evolution and comparative religion. His classes were standing room only. People would come to Sunday School who hadn't been to church in years. He could go to church for that and for the choir. It was during this time that Darrel realized how manipulative religion is. One Sunday he chose the schmaltziest solo he could think of and sang for the congregation...bringing many to tears. His hypothesis was proven: ministers use music to manipulate congregations.

By the time he was 32, he believed there was "no sky daddy up there" but was not ready to make a definitive statement about it. By 38 he was making the definitive statement. Being agnostic says 'I'm not sure that there is any god, but I'm not going to put my bets down.' An atheist says they're 99% sure. Darrel admits that no one is going to claim they're 100% certain, but atheists are 99% sure.

The only common thread that ties all atheists together

is a lack of belief in gods and supernatural beings. Some of the best debates he has ever had have been with fellow atheists. This is because atheists do not have a common belief system, sacred scripture or atheist leader. This means atheists often disagree on many issues and ideas. Atheists come in a variety of shapes, colors, beliefs, convictions, and backgrounds. They are as unique as their fingerprints.

Darrel has some fascinating beliefs as it pertains to an afterlife, and that religions use the belief in an afterlife as yet another means of manipulating and controlling people. He believes there are two concepts in religion: there is a heaven and a hell, hell being the stronger of the two. We're scared to death of hell and don't want to go there. Why do you need the concept of hell unless you want to control people? Hell has been the most useful debilitating mental concept that will make people do horrendous things in the name of their god. Yet the mere belief in heaven doesn't mean one can define the criteria for getting there.

The pope recently said even atheists could potentially be in heaven. This lack of clarity allows for incredible emotional and psychological manipulation. How can people say they're comforted by the idea of going to heaven when they don't know what it takes to get there? There have been people sainted by the Catholic Church who are horrendous people...some who participated in the Spanish Inquisition, for instance. So when someone says they have a faith that gives them comfort in the possibility of being in heaven, Darrel says they're delusional. No one can define how to get there or what it's like, and every religion thinks they're the only ones who are going to heaven.

Darrel expressed concern about people's views of an afterlife and refers to what he calls the toxic trio:

1. Belief in an afterlife
2. Belief in a voyeuristic all-knowing god who determines your status in the afterlife
3. Belief that the god dictates a specific type of behavior as a condition of entry into the afterlife

When his psychologist ears hear someone say they have a faith in the afterlife, he hears debilitating cognitive concepts. In his practice, the more religious you are the more you use religion as an excuse for not doing what you need to do. For instance, how much time is wasted praying for something rather than just doing it? 'I've been praying for a job' vs. just searching for a job. Praying for heath vs. exercising and making healthy food choices. Praying for grades vs. working with a tutor. There's no concrete evidence that prayer works, but there _are_ coincidences. A man prays for work and gets a job…he can't prove he wouldn't have gotten the job anyway. We see pro football players kneeling and raising their arms skyward after making a touchdown as if to say that God blessed him with the extra points. Darrel points out that thousands of children in Africa are dying of dreaded diseases that one praying athlete could cure if he donated a part of his salary. But he'd rather pray than do something positive for other human beings.

Darrel wants to point out how people are wasting time praying in church instead of doing what they could do to improve their lives. One of the most economically depressed places in the country is Mississippi, which is also one of the most religious. In Darrel's opinion, there is a significant correlation between religiosity and achievement.

He asks that we look at the achievement of religious people. Thomas Edison was an atheist, and we have five atheists to thank for the internet and the computer. He contends we would be much more productive. If we spent our church time learning how to do math or accounting better, we would be dedicating time to something productive rather than listening to a preacher who's trying to get 10% of our income.

Atheists are generous people. They need no promise of an eternal life being held over their heads to force them to behave in kind, supportive ways toward their fellow man. Quite the contrary…this is the only life they have, so they want to be sure they're doing their best while they're here. Because of a belief in afterlife, people are giving money that's being misused. Darrel's approach to life is quite simple: "I'm going to do the best I can with what I've got now." In his work with Recovering from Religion, he hears people who leave religion often say they feel liberated. There's no god watching over their shoulder, and they have no fear that they're going to burn in hell. They can spend mental energy doing things for their family that they weren't doing before. They go to college; they use their money more productively. Atheists get a 10% bonus when leaving church and Sunday mornings to sleep in.

Darrel says the fear of death is a Christian myth and that all religions want you to be scared. None of us wants to die, but being afraid is something else. Dying is the problem rather than death. Not long ago an Atheist friend found out he was dying. He called a few friends to come out so they could have a four-day weekend celebrating his life. It was one of the most cathartic experiences of his life. Everyone was at peace. The probability of our existence is so tiny that we should be grateful to have one shot at this life…. much less a life for eternity. Do the best you can while you're alive. Mark Twain says this of an afterlife: "I do not fear death. I had been dead for billions and billions of years before I was born, and had not suffered the slightest inconvenience from it."

If you don't do exactly what god says, you're going to hell. People who haven't gone to church in decades are still afraid of going to hell, and that fear frames their behavior toward people. Homosexuals (or whatever goes against their cultural expectations or religious beliefs) are going to hell. Belief in an afterlife gives people permission to condemn and abuse other people, gives you permission to abuse your own children and indoctrinate them. Children have even been killed by parents in the name of religion...beaten senseless and terrorized by parents telling them they're going to hell if they step out of line. Darrel's own grandmother told him he was going to hell for misbehaving. Religion and the belief in an afterlife are a license to abuse children. Darrel's dad beat him when he questioned a bible verse. Because of your own terror of the afterlife...and the fear that you will be held responsible for your child going to hell...you "discipline" your children. According to Darrel's research, the number one predictor of child abuse in a family is drug/alcohol abuse. Number two is religiosity. Darrel says, "We acquire both the language and religious concepts from our immediate culture – at the same time. A child cannot discriminate between useful survival information and the emotional and psychological manipulations of religion. Once infected, these ideas are deeply embedded and almost impossible to change."

KEEP YOUR FORK

Darrel's road to atheism has been long and winding… starting with his fundamental Christian upbringing to his current anti-religion stance. The road took turns for his family of origin as well. By the end of his parents' lives, there was no religiosity at all. The last three days of his dad's life…as he lost his battle with colorectal cancer…were great days of laughing and joking. Not one person mentioned religion. Nobody talked about heaven or hell or rewards of a life that awaited him. When he died, Darrel went to the preacher and told him there would be no proselytizing or he'd stand and interrupt the service. The preacher was free to talk about his dad in religious terms but no proselytizing to use his dad's death to get new members of his church. He had the same conversation when his mom passed three years later.

Darrel doesn't have to believe there's a god who loves him so much he'll banish him to hell forever if he falls short in some way. No one can tell him for sure what to do to get to heaven. Catholics say one thing, Mormons another, Muslims yet another. He has no idea what to do to get to this place called heaven. An academic at heart, the lack of concrete proof and criteria for gaining entry prevent him from buying into the religious hype surrounding eternal glory or damnation.

There are thousands of groups that will get you into

religion; Darrel's group is the only one that will help you get out. Some end up being agnostic; some become pagan or new age. His group wants to help people get over the trauma of religious indoctrination, proffering,

> *"Religion has the capacity to silence critical thinking and create blindness in entire groups of people."*

Darrel finds being an atheist to be liberating. There's no god out there judging them so he can send them to hell. They can just enjoy themselves. But when questioned as to where accountability comes into play if there is no one "watching," Darrel shared a simple statistic: .4% of all people in prison are atheists. Most of the people in prison are Christians (Baptists have the highest percentage of the prison population). Who are the most educated and most economically successful in the United States? Atheists. Because they're focused on this experience, and education is the only way to make this experience the best it can be. Darrel believes we have one shot at life: doing good, being productive, taking accountability for your own experience…that's what matters.

The default position is that there is no heaven or hell. Heaven and hell are products of later man-made cultures. All atheists have done is to go back to the default position. It's not a "belief". No, Christians have a belief that there is a heaven or hell; Darrel sees no evidence of it, so he considers it null and void. Don't accuse him of having a belief about something that doesn't exist. "I don't believe in cultural constructs that have no evidence."

Darrel's story is certainly not going to sway everyone because God-belief has been indoctrinated into our society for a long time, and most people have been raised to believe in some deity or another since before they could walk. But perhaps it may cause you to ponder your deeply held faith-based convictions.

The Bible is the foundation for a Christian life, but even mainstream Christians will tell you that it is full of contradictions that are open to multiple interpretations. Ever since the dawn of time, religions have been fighting a losing battle against science. God has moved more and more to the gaps of human understanding. There was a time when if humanity didn't know the answer to one of life's questions, then God was that answer. That time apparently is still the present but fortunately, science is providing more and more answers.

A major point in atheism supporting the lack of a deity is the suffering we see and experience every day. One might ask: did the starving children in Africa offend God in some way? Perhaps those kids need to suffer horribly and die to teach us something important. What about all the people who have cancer? Does God have his reasons for torturing them? The existence of evil and suffering continues to be a compelling argument for atheism.

The reality is that there is no concrete evidence for any deities. If there were valid and compelling evidence, then we would all be on the same page. There wouldn't be thousands of sects of each religion and there wouldn't be innumerable different religions. There would be one sect of one religion and God would make His presence known to us in a way that was so obvious that it couldn't be disputed. We would be able to see Him, hear Him, smell Him, touch Him, etc. There would be no atheists because we would have no choice but to believe.

Based on Darrel's premise, we might all then consider ourselves agnostics. We don't know whether any deities exist. There is no evidence for the existence of any deities. There is no good reason to believe that any deities actually exist. So without any valid reason to believe that any deities exist, he doesn't believe any deities exist. And because we are agnostic, we should also be atheists.

Food for thought? Or just worm food?

KEEP YOUR FORK

Dirt Cake

Ingredients

Clean medium-sized flower pot and plastic wrap
1 box chocolate sandwich cookies
2 3.9 oz. packages instant chocolate pudding
3½ cups milk
8 oz. cream cheese, softened
2 8-10 oz. containers frozen whipped topping, thawed
A few gummy worms

Preparation

- Wash the flower pot with soap and warm water. Dry, and line with plastic wrap. If the flower pot has a hole at the bottom, place it on a clean dish.
- Place chocolate sandwich cookies in a food processor, fitted with a metal blade. Pulse until the cookies become coarse crumbs.
- Whisk together chocolate pudding and milk until thick and pudding like. Chill while making the cream cheese mixture.
- Beat cream cheese with an electric mixer until fluffy. Beat in 1 container of thawed whipped topping until smooth. Add the cream cheese mixture to the chocolate pudding mixture, mixing until smooth.
- Place a layer of the cookie crumbs in the bottom of the lined flower pot. Top with a layer of the chocolate pudding mixture. Continue making layers of the dirt cake: the cookie crumbs, then the

chocolate pudding mixture, until there is about 1 inch left at the top. ***Note: Be sure to leave plenty of cookie crumbs for the top - you can't have a dirt cake without a lot of dirt!***
- Spread the remaining container of thawed whipped topping over the last layer of chocolate pudding, and top with the remaining cookie crumbs. Place a few gummy worms on the dirt cake. Cover with plastic wrap and refrigerate until ready to serve.

Everlasting Life

*For God so loved the world
that he gave his only begotten Son,
that whosoever believeth in him should not perish,
but have everlasting life.*
—John 3:16

EVERLASTING LIFE

When the topic of religion and heaven comes up, it's hard not to go back to your roots and really think about where your beliefs originated. Misty's childhood friends Kathryn Adams and her twin sister Becky led her to Christ as a youth. In her early teens they convinced her and her entire family to go to the small country church where their father was the minister, Ocheltree Baptist. Their love for music and faith in the Almighty was a powerful example and ultimately influenced Misty to ask God into her heart. Because of this, Misty knew that Kathryn would have a fantastic testimony about heaven.

When we arrived at Kathryn's (which by the way is not what Misty called her as a kid; it was simply Kathy back then), she was engaged in the duties of being a mother. With her young son Caleb on her hip, she was the perfect hostess, offering us tea and presenting a plate of home-made cookies. We spent a bit of time catching up on each other's families and recent life events. After assuring us that her entire life is boring and that she will have nothing really inspiring to offer, we dove into the topic of heaven.

> *"Well, I guess I have to start by saying I believe we'll be in heaven because I think that's incredibly important. And even though I was raised in a Baptist family with a minister as a father, it was still my choice. It wasn't just forced*

> *on me. I was brought to church and taught the Bible. Regardless of whom your parents are and the influence they have over you, there is a point where you have to make decision to love God on your own. It was in my early 20's that I made the decision I was going to follow Christ because it was my choice.*
>
> *I will say that because of my beliefs if you don't ever make a decision and do something about it, you're not going to go heaven. I think for me it's important for people to understand why I'm going to heaven; it's because I did ask Christ into my heart, I confessed my sins and I do believe those things are essential. I believe that Jesus Christ lived a sinless life, was crucified on the cross to take away my sins and rose from the dead."*

Kathryn takes her role as a Christian parent seriously. She hopes and prays that Caleb will come to a conclusion that God is all he wants, based on what he's experienced with his parents. But until Caleb gets to that point, it's Kathryn's responsibility to teach him as her parents taught her. Just as she made the decision to follow Christ…not because it was her parents' wish for her, but because it was what she chose to do.

EVERLASTING LIFE

"Now that I am a parent I hope that the things that my husband and I are teaching Caleb and investing in him will lead to the conclusion that God is good and it's important to live a life that honors Him. I know for a fact God is part of my life because of the personal experiences I have had with Him, but until Caleb gets to the point to understand that on his own, it's my responsibility to teach him just as it was my parents responsibility to teach me."

Everything she believes and how she lives is because of the Bible, especially her choice to follow Christ. She says it started back in the Garden of Eden. When God created Adam and Eve, He intended for us to have fellowship with somebody because He didn't have fellowship. Unfortunately, Satan came along, tempted them, they fell for it, and then sin came into the world. So there had to be a way to get to heaven. At that point, they had what is referred to as Purgatory, which is attained by works because the blood had not been shed for the remission of sins. But then when Christ came and lived a sinless life, the opportunity to choose was created. It's not enough to believe that; you have to act on it. Because the Bible says that you have to confess your sins and you have to ask Him into your heart. You go to heaven because you have accepted Him. But if you don't make that decision and do something about it, you won't be spending eternity with Jesus.

KEEP YOUR FORK

If you look in the Bible clearly, there are three heavens mentioned. One heaven is here on earth, the earthly kingdom. The second heaven is what we as NASA try to find in outer space. And the third heaven is where God resides. She casually interrupts herself to wonder if somehow NASA is trying to get to that third heaven. Again looking to the Bible, Kathryn reminds us that there's a battle with Satan for a kingdom and God is going to protect what He has created. God didn't want to create hell, but there has to be some place for people to go if they choose to reject His Son. God makes a way for each of us to get there because God's love is overwhelming.

It's hard for Kathryn to think that people don't believe in God and don't believe in heaven.

> *"I guess the way that I view heaven, there's a lot of things that you can look at heaven, I mean, scripturally you can know that there are streets of gold and that there's 12 gates for the 12 tribes of Israel and that the gate itself is one big pearl and there's all these precious stones. There are 12 specifically precious stones. I can't imagine their beauty. I mean, we think a little pearl this big is beautiful. I mean, I can't imagine how big this gate will be and I can't imagine gold being what we walk on, you know. When I get tired of the new tar they lay*

down that ends up on my car, I think I'd be happy with gold on my car."

Earth is just part of our journey, but what we do on earth determines what we'll do in heaven. The Bible makes that very clear. And it doesn't mean our position or role. It doesn't mean if you're a doctor that's better than if you wash dishes at McDonald's. It's doing what God instructs us, and not the earthly things that we do but the spiritual things. Are you giving an encouraging word? Are you showing the love of Christ. Are you forgiving when you've been hurt? And to whom much is given, much is required to give back.

Kathryn spends time in communion with God every day, in prayer and reading the Bible, because she wants to know what He wants her to do for the day. She believes if she's to represent Christ, she has to represent Him in everything she does. Even if it's stopping to help an old lady with her car. One day recently as Kathryn was leaving her neighborhood, she noticed a little old lady standing on the side of the street trying to do something with her gas cap. And she thought, "Somebody needs to help this lady." Granted, she got it fixed by the time Kathryn got her car stopped and got out; but still, she wonders why in our society why we are not doing more of that. Kathryn thinks it's because we're so self-focused that we don't see beyond what our next thing is to look for ways to show kindness.

> *"I have learned with my walk with Christ is I try to have a heaven-bound focus, but where I do a check, a reality check. Is it really going to matter in heaven? When I'm on my deathbed, will it matter what purse I carried? No. Will it matter what car I drove? No. Will it matter that I invested in other people? Yes. Will it matter that I fed the poor? Yes. Will it matter that I shared the gospel? Yes. Those things will matter. And so I really do try to focus on those things. I am not perfect by any means. I make mistakes. I sin. I do those things, but I know for me I really do think about that because I don't want to live with regrets."*

Kathryn believes God doesn't send anybody to hell. We choose; it's our choice. We either choose Christ or choose nothing; and choosing nothing destines you to an eternity in hell. While not believing in a fire-and-brimstone fear-based God, she also believes in a healthy fear of God. Though there are three heavens, this earth-bound life is not heaven for Kathryn. This is not what God intended for our life when He created Adam and Eve. He created us to be able to sing and to praise all day. When she reaches her ultimate destination in the arms of Jesus, she hopes to walk on water. She imagines tasting things we've never tasted before. She won't have happiness or sadness because there won't be such feelings there…only joy. Colors will be beyond any words we have to describe them. Our world was created by God to include great color, and Kathryn took a moment to ponder what God's favorite color might be. Is it blue or green? We have the beautiful blue sky above, and the earth is covered in shades of green. When we all get to heaven we will see God for his true glory. We will truly understand the trinity.

> *"I've studied the trinity. I understand God the Father. I understand God the Son. I understand the Holy Spirit. I understand they are three in one. I still cannot grasp the concept fully, you know what I mean? I mean, I understand because the Holy Spirit has convicted me at times. I know the Holy Spirit has revoked things to me at times. I know that the Holy Spirit guides me. I know, I know that I have heard the still small voice of God. It was not loud. It was not audible. But the Bible talks about the still small voice where I knew that I knew that's what God wanted me to do and said things, you know. And, again, it was nothing against the word of God. It went with the word of God. I think you have to be careful about hearing God's voice. I'll be honest with you about that. But that only comes from a relationship with God. But when we get to heaven, we're going to see."*

KEEP YOUR FORK

Although Kathryn is a busy working mom, she does take time to read her Bible. But no matter how much time she spends in the Word, God always reveals something new and fresh. So one day when she gets to heaven she believes everything will make sense because she's read the "owner's manual." Kathryn is clearly well-grounded in the Bible, but she also admits she won't be surprised if, when she gets to heaven, she'll have to wonder why she didn't know more. Because she wants to know Christ so well that she will recognize Him when she sees Him face to face. Not just because of His glory, but because she knows His character. And because she knows Him as her friend and savior.

"There only two things that will last for eternity: the word of God and the souls of people."

As part of Kathryn's work as a pediatric dental hygienist, she has done many mission trips providing dental care to those in need in Peru, Mexico and El Salvador. Kathryn says the one thing she's learned from the perspective of other people is that everybody knows that there's a higher power and everyone seeks that in the depths of their souls. God makes a way for each of us to get there because God's love is overwhelming.

"I honestly do not know how people can walk through this life without Christ. I really

don't because let's face it, life is hard, I believe society right now looks at God like a genie in a bottle. If you rub him, pray to him, and ask could you do this for me, then our "prayers" will come true. I believe that this is just a journey; earth is just part of the journey, but that journey helps determine what we'll do in heaven. The Bible makes that very clear. And it doesn't mean the position or the role. It doesn't mean if you're a doctor that's better than if you wash dishes at McDonald's. It's what God instructs us to do and it's not the earthly things it's spiritual. Are you giving an encouraging word? Are you showing the love of Christ? Are you forgiving when you've been hurt? We were made to worship Him. We were made to bring Him glory. If you are given much, much will be required of you. If much is entrusted to you, much will be expected of you. (Luke 12:48)"

When asked who she'd like to meet in heaven (aside from Jesus, of course), she said it would be amazing to sit down and talk to Moses. And she would like to talk to Elizabeth; she wonders how it felt to be so old. But the person she most wants to talk to is Sarah because she was having kids at 90 years of age. Kathryn had a difficult pregnancy that came relatively later in life, and due to her age she developed gestational diabetes. So during her pregnancy when she experienced problems, she thought of Sarah. She must have had this, and it had to have been worse…after all, she was twice Kathryn's age! And with a twinkle in her eye and a grin on her face, she admitted she'd love to meet Eve so she could slap her "for that monthly gift."

Kathryn's story is powerful; she does not in any way question her faith. She lives it and breathes it every day without question. That in itself is what makes her story such a commanding testimony. During the time we spent with Kathryn, it's not hard to imagine that God was shining down on her and letting His spirit come through.

As we prepared to leave, Kathryn said, "I told you I would be the most boring interview." We think she was very wrong.

Imagine

For to be free is not merely to cast off one's chains,
but to live in a way that respects
and enhances the freedom of others.
—Nelson Mandela

IMAGINE

When Margie and I first started this project I had a very clear vision in my mind. Take some pictures; get some funny thought provoking stories, a few recipes and ta-da we would have a book. In many ways that is what we accomplished, but there really was so much more to it. I've had the opportunity to meet so many amazing people and hear their stories. In fact, it inspired me to share my own story. I hope you enjoy it.

Growing up in a Baptist family, I heard a lot about heaven and hell. Heaven seemed like a better opportunity than hell, plus I really hate being hot! So as a child I lived by the lessons I'd been taught from the Bible and loved every moment of it. I was on fire for God like many new Christians, and I wanted only to please Him. I wanted to sing about His glory and give my life completely to God. "Make this your one purpose: to revere Him and serve Him faithfully with complete devotion because He has done great things for you." (1 Samuel 12:24) And I think all of that would have been possible if it hadn't been for one small problem: I like girls.

For a long time I felt as if the path leading to God had been chained and locked up tight. I had to put my faith away because if I was gay, God wouldn't... couldn't...love me. I was damaged and unworthy of His love, and this broke my heart. Over time, I started to realize that God had never stopped loving me. This whole time I had been blaming God for not loving me when the truth was He had never stopped. I'm the one who had created the chains. I'm the one who locked the gate that led to my peace and freedom. I was so caught up in the lip service of "people" that I stopped listening to the voice that mattered most. "And He will be leading you. He'll be with you, and He'll never fail you or abandon you. So don't be afraid!" (Deuteronomy 31:8)

So now the "Big J.C." and I are on good terms. I live how I live and if "people" don't like it, oh well. And with that in mind, here is my view of heaven/the afterlife/the best is yet to come. I don't necessarily know what it will look like or feel like, but that doesn't stop me from imagining. Sometimes I hope it will be like a choose-your-own-adventure book where each day I can continue to learn and grow. I'd like there to be a 24-hour buffet that has whatever food I want at the time and an endless supply of fresh crab that has already been taken out of the shell. I'd also enjoy endless karaoke with great singers, friends and laughter and to have a smoking hot body that looks like Shakira, because her "hips don't lie"! But the most important thing I will want in heaven is my wife Michele. I spent so long looking for her; I just don't want to waste a single moment without her. I want to hold her hand while drinking pineapple mimosas and dance together in white sand and turquoise water.

IMAGINE

This is my dream, my faith, my hope. That's the beauty of this life; we each have the free will to choose what we believe. I found that during the interviews for this book, regardless of each person's view on the afterlife, everyone always got around to how we treat each other as a society and the importance of being kind and loving one another. "And above all things, have fervent charity among yourselves, for charity shall cover the multitude of sins." (1 Peter 4:8) Ultimately I think this book represents the best of what we all want: to be loved and accepted by someone or something.

Peace be with you my friends. May we meet on the other side!

Misty Town

Funeral Potatoes

Ingredients

1 package (32 ounces) frozen cubed hash brown potatoes, thawed
1 pound process cheese (Velveeta), cubed
2 cups (16 ounces) sour cream
1 can (10-3/4 ounces) condensed cream of chicken soup, undiluted
3/4 cup butter, melted, divided
3 tablespoons chopped onion
1/4 teaspoon paprika
1/2 teaspoon salt
1/4 teaspoon pepper
2 cups cornflakes, lightly crushed

Directions

- In a large bowl, combine the hash browns, cheese, sour cream, soup, 1/2 cup butter and onion.
- Spread into a greased 13x9-in. baking dish.
- Sprinkle with paprika.
- Combine cornflakes and remaining butter; sprinkle on top.
- Bake, covered, at 350° for 40-50 minutes or until heated through. Uncover, bake 10 minutes longer or until top is golden brown.

Bibliography

Scripture quotations taken from the 21ˢᵗ Century King James Version®, copyright© 1994. Used by permission of Deuel Enterprises, Inc. Gary, SD 57237. All rights reserved.